SOLO TENNIS

SOLO TENNIS

By
Virginia Yale
and
Morey Lewis

DRAKE PUBLISHERS INC.
NEW YORK • LONDON

V

Published in 1976 by
DRAKE PUBLISHERS INC.
801 Second Avenue
New York, N.Y. 10017

ISBN: 0-8473-1062-0
LC: 75-36142

Printed in The United States of America

PREFACE

Morey Lewis was one of the better players on the circuit in the late 1930's. As a member of the Kenyon College team which won the Intercollegiate Championship in 1939, he wrecked havoc on many higher ranked players. He started to perfect his sound, all-around game on a backboard in Texarkana, Texas.

In his book, SOLO TENNIS, he makes available to the new tennis player, youngster and oldster alike, the basic skills of proper grips and shows how to develop sound swings to execute groundstrokes, volleys and other strokes with which to build a winning game. Interestingly enough, he shows how to do it all using a backboard!

It's an excellent book for beginners and I highly recommend it.

—*Bill Talbert*

CONTENTS

SOLO TENNIS

Chapter One

A BACKBOARD BELIEVER

To most people, a backboard is dead weight, (not to mention ugly) and should be removed from grounds of private or public tennis clubs. However, Morey Lewis, who is a past Arkansas State Champion, Canadian Champion twice, and Champion of the state of California, will swiftly challenge you to a duel if you suggest it.

To Morey, the backboard is not dead weight, nor is it ugly. He believes it is the backbone of a tennis winner. He thinks most tennis players have a yen to win, and a yen lacking knowledge is foolish.

"Using the backboard gives you in depth knowledge while edging you toward the WINNER'S CUP," Morey explains.

"Tennis is not only for the young," he declares. Humphrey Bogart may have uttered the memorable line, "Tennis, anyone?" But it is Morey Lewis who asks, "SOLO TENNIS-ANYONE?" He has many takers of all ages.

When Morey was in high school, he lived in a small town—Horatio, Arkansas. The only tennis players were his mother, father, Aunt Sue and Uncle Fred. He knew there was an Arkansas high school tournament. He knew he could beat anyone in Horatio. He knew he could WIN that tournament. He entered.

Since horatio did not have the tree of knowledge on tennis protocol, Morey was soon to learn that he was wet behind the ears in this area.

His first embarrassment was his first lesson in tennis etiquette. When he arrived at the tournament, he was not dressed in white, starchy tennis togs—a "must" in those days; instead, he was in coveralls with high-top basketball shoes. However, his most painful humiliation was his smashing defeat of 6-0; 6-0. He was so embarrassed, he bought his own trophy to take home. His father never said a word; however, every day his father would look at the trophy and laugh. Then one day his father asked, "Morey, are you SERIOUS about learning to play tennis?"

"Of course," exclaimed Morey.

"Then I'll give you a backboard."

His father did. Morey learned to play tennis—SOLO—on the backboard. The backboard taught him enough to win the title of tennis champion several times. Later in life he dropped from the tennis circuit for twenty-three years. Because of health problems and his extreme interest in development of youth in tennis, he left his profession of mechanical and chemical engineer to teach tennis. He taught in Little Rock Arkansas; Pine Bluff, Arkansas; and Dallas, Texas. Now he is manager and tennis "pro" at Tyler Tennis and Swim Club in Tyler, Texas.

Morey has developed a youth program in Tyler that includes ages from 6 to 20. There are 105 local members. Out-of-town members total 60, coming from Arkansas, Louisiana and surrounding towns—large and small. He is known as the Pied Piper of the young. All of his students, whether in his youth program or his adult classes, are taught the importance of the tennis backboard. His philosophy is PRACTICE—on the backboard, as well as the court.

Morey claims you can learn all the basic strokes of tennis on the backboard, with the exception of two—the lob and the service return. He says, "The five basic strokes are: (1) forehand; (2) backhand; (3) volley; (4) service; (5) smash-plus sly 'foxy' shots, half-volley drop shot and slice."

"Fifteen minutes practice a day on backboard," he adds, "with previous adequate instruction, will turn you from a 'dainty dubber' to a 'wise winner'."

"This is true," he says, "because when you practice on the backboard, you hit the same shots so many times they become automatic—as automatic as putting your key in your car before you start it."

Then he explains, "You don't think, 'I must put key in the ignition.' You automatically do it. This is what the tennis backboard teaches you. You become smooth and easy."

"On occasions," Morey explains, "I will find those who accept my challenge to a duel regarding the effectiveness of the backboard practice. They claim it is not realistic tennis."

With a twinkle in his eye and a grin on his face, he hurriedly adds, "I don't buy that. I know better." He claims the ball machine spits the ball at the same pace and almost same spot, and does not give enough contrast in practice.

He says that the advantage of backboard practice enables you to overcome your weakness and teaches the basic essentials—balance, shifting weight from rear to front foot, eye on the ball, concentration, timing, position of racket at time of impact and the racket follow-through. Once these fundamentals have been accomplished, the player will have a sound foundation for the game and will be ready for swift, serious competition on the tennis court.

"SOLO TENNIS practice on backboard does not exclude court practice, Morey explains. Backboard practice makes you hit more balls—thus more practice."

Next, he explains the ground strokes. A ground stroke is when your racket clashes with a charging ball after ball has bounded once. Two important points for your ground strokes are (1) racket back, weight forward and swing; and (2) start with the racket head back low and finish the stroke with the racket head high above your head.

"Memorize these two fundamentals and PRACTICE them on the tennis backboard," Morey advises.

As you progress through this book, Morey is going to illustrate the five basic strokes and plus factors. He will give you adequate instructions on how to practice on the tennis backboard. However, before you do this, you must learn the hand grips for your tennis racket.

There are three basic grips, the first being the Eastern grip. This grip is called the "shaking hand" grip, because your hand shakes hands with the racket's handle. Your wrist will be behind the racket's handle, giving the stroke more power. For the Eastern backhand grip, slip the thumb in back of the handle.

The second grip is the Continental. It is like the Eastern forehand, only the hand is edged slightly to the left of the racket's handle. This grip is excellent for slice-volley-smash-lob-drop shots, but the Continental grip specializes in service.

The third grip is the Western grip, the least popular among the pros. Lay your racket flat on the ground and grip the racket's handle.

Now that TV gives tennis "prime time," watch the pros' grips. The TV camera will zero in on many shots. Test yourself—see if you can recognize the grips. No cheating! Remember, tennis is a "gentleman's game."

"However," states Morey, "there is nothing absolute about these three grips. Everyone has his own variation. Just be sure to adjust the grip for your hand. Remember, the grip and wrist add POWER."

Haydite Tennis Backboard

Racket Back

Weight Forward and Swing

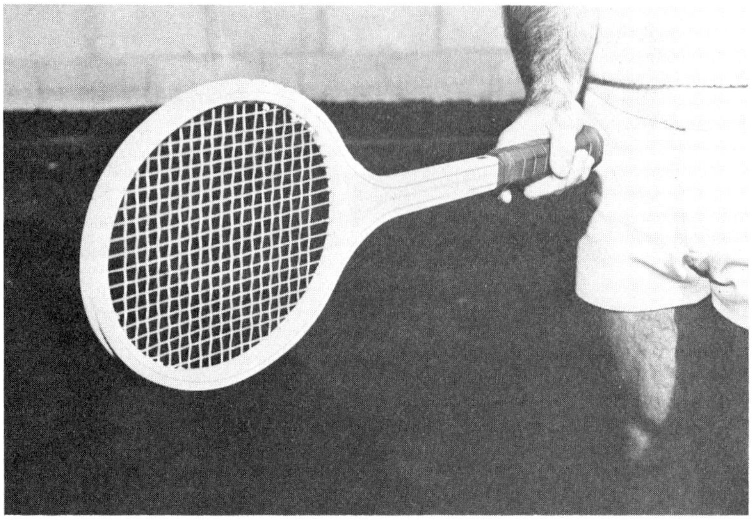

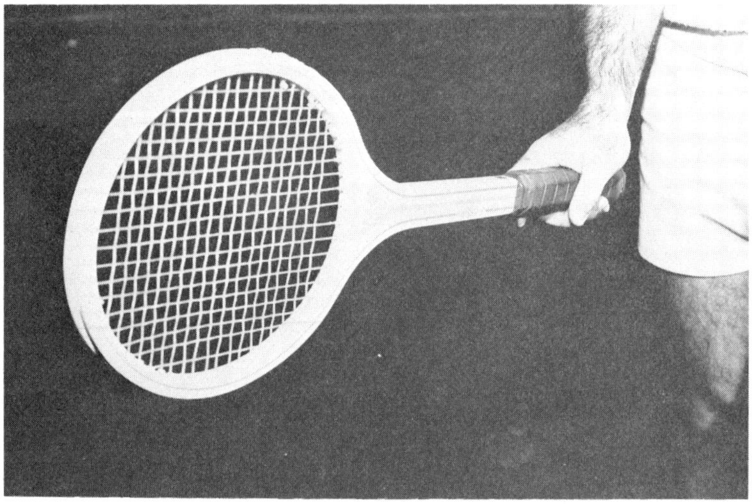

(Top) The Eastern Grip

(Center) The Continental Grip

(Bottom) The Western Grip

Chapter Two

YESTERYEAR'S—TODAY'S—TOMORROW'S—TENNIS

To compare yesteryear's tennis to doday's tennis, you will find the attire, the equipment and the court surface are as different as a lion and a canary. As an example, in 1874 when Mary Outerbridge first brought tennis to America, the ladies donned the courts in tennis attire in keeping with the styles of the day. They wore a long white dress dangling slightly above their ankles with several starched petticoats beneath the dress, a tight corset at their waists, with a full bustle at the back of the dress. Their figures were like an hourglass. Their hair was tucked neatly under a shadowing brim hat, while they skipped nimbly across the courts in their high-topped buttoned white shoes—always a white handkerchief to blot their moistened brow.

Yesteryear's debonairish tennis gentlemen wore long, loose white slacks, a blazer or coat, a white shirt with a small bow tie, and plain shoes. Their head was usually topped with a derby or cap. They probably would have been just as comfortable going to work in their "suit" like tennis attire.

However, the attire of the gracious antebellum days with its long, bustled dress and the "suited" look for men have disappeared. Today's tennis clothing is more comfortable and pragmatic. Tennis clothing manufacturers have yielded to "today's" fast, competitive game and stock tennis shops with comfortable tennis clothes for fast action.

Today's female tennis players have dropped the tight corsets, the bulksome bustles and the high-top buttoned white shoes. As they dash and dart around the tennis courts, the women dress in one-piece short tennis dresses or short tennis skirts and comfortable blouses. If she has a trim figure, she may wear tennis shorts and a blouse. Today her tennis wardrobe may be of several colors instead of only white, as was yesteryear's. However, white is still the most acceptable color, expecially for tournaments.

Since their feet are their way of traveling around the tennis courts, tennis shoes are the most important part of tennis attire. There are brands of tennis shoes or sneakers made expecially for tennis play. A plain, flat, thin-soled tennis shoe is *not* enough. They are not padded enough to protect her feet from the hot surface, should she play in hot weather. The regular brand tennis shoe will have thick soles, slightly ribbed to keep her from sliding. Some tennis shoes have supported arches and heels.

Today's female tennis player's feet will not be covered with yesteryear's silk stockings, but rather with thick socks that absorb moisture. Neither will she wear a large brim hat. Today, *if* she wears anything on her head, it will be a sun visor or a cap to keep the sun out of her eyes.

Today's male tennis player dresses in tennis shorts, or slacks, should it be cool, with a polo shirt or sport shirt—no tie. Today he, too, may color his wardrobe to match the color of his eyes, should he so desire.

"However, as with the women, in BIG championship play, white is always right," states Morey.

Men playing tennis today leave their "plain shoes" on the shoe shelf and scamper about the courts with regular brand tennis shoes and socks, as do the women.

Today, if it is chilly on the courts, both men and women will be seen in colored "warm up" suits—adding rainbow colors to the busy courts.

Out of yesteryear's halls of tennis history—Major Wingfield claimed he invented the game of tennis and received a patent for his game in February, 1974. The design of his court dimensions and net height were different from today's court dimensions.

Today's court surface is rectangular, with a smaller surface for the player to dash around on. Too, the net is lower. Yesteryear's court surface

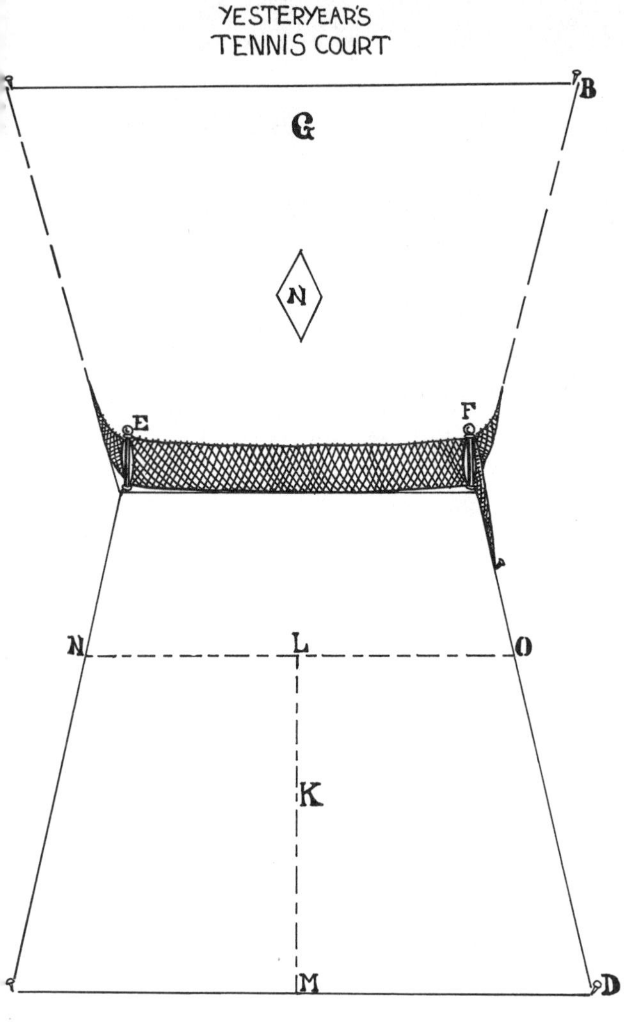

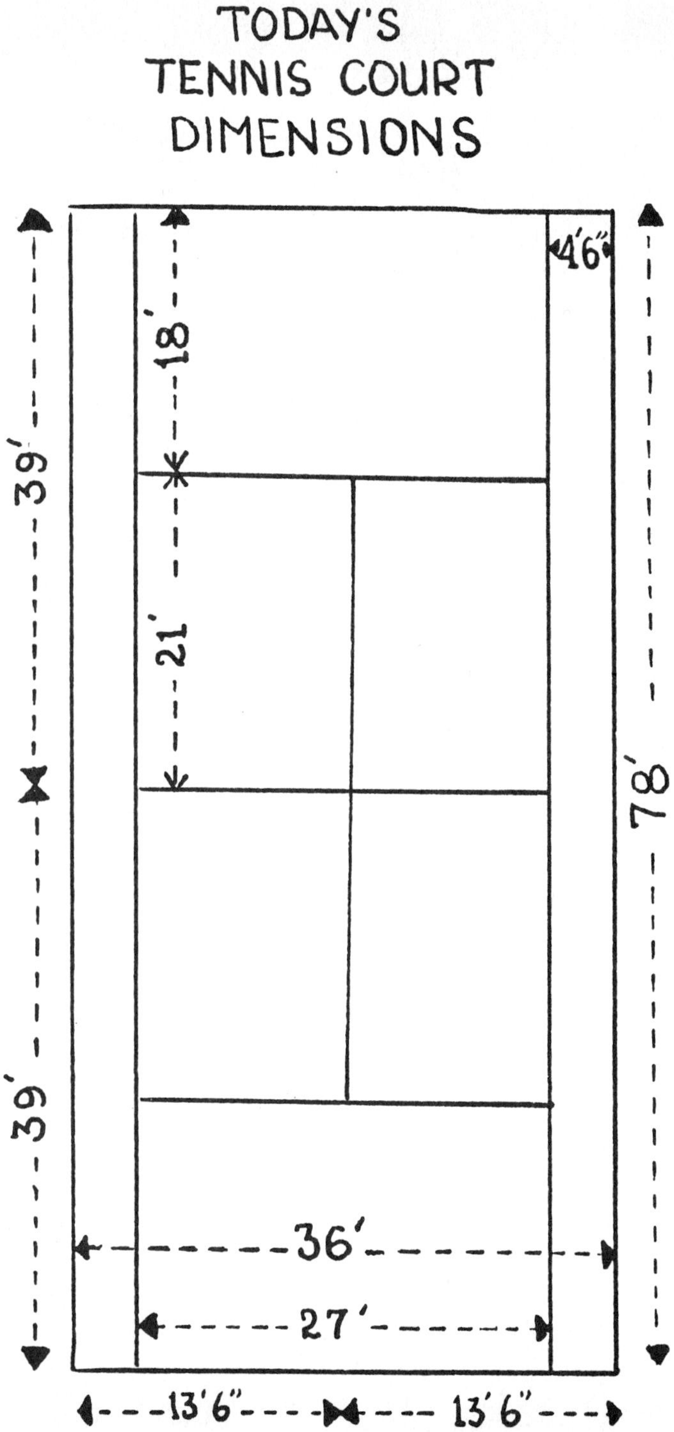

TODAY'S NET IS 3½ FEET AT NET POST and 3 FEET IN CENTER

Today's Tennis Attire

was grass. Today's court surfaces have many varieties—as many varieties as the player has in his choice of tennis rackets. Today's surface may be grass, clay, a type of cement; it may be a fast surface or a slow surface.

"Tomorrow's equipment may be different from yesteryear's and today's. The materials may be more exotic. As an example, the materials for tennis rackets may be made from graphite. They might develop a racket string that will equal today's gut string. It will take time, but they will do it." Morey declares.

They may work out a change in ball compression—possibly a slow ball for a fast court and a fast ball for a slow court. Some believe the surface dimensions of tomorrow's tennis may be changed.

"The biggest change in tomorrow's tennis will be the acceptance of a standard court surface. There are too many varieties, and as players head out of town for tennis weekends, they find too many changes in the courts' surfaces," states Morey.

Too, tomorrow's tennis will have more enclosed courts. The advantages of enclosed courts will automatically bring this about. Your conditions are perfect—temperature and lighting are good. As an example, Morey explains, "When you have an indoor tournament and they play at two o'clock in the morning, the court is in the same condition as it was at three o'clock in the afternoon, or ten o'clock in the morning, or four o'clock in the morning." Enclosed courts will be the "IN" thing in tomorrow's tennis.

The Virginia Slim, Womens' Tennis Circuit, released the news of using a new electronic sensing system that automatically calls the close shots. The system is called the Electronic Line Judge, invented by Dr. Geof Grant. Morey believes the electronic machine for line calling will be used in tomorrow's game, but mainly in the championship tournaments and not in the regular tournaments all over the country.

Because many championship matches are being televised, time becomes a factor. Morey believes tomorrow's tennis will drop the add and deuce and go to a four point game—15-30-40 game.

(Left) Position for forehand stroke
(Bottom, Left) Weight moves forward on left foot
(Below) Finish forehand stroke with racket high

Chapter Three

HOW TO TEACH YOURSELF TENNIS ON BACKBOARD

"Before you march to the backboard, remember previous, adequate instruction is a MUST," warns Morey.

Assuming you have had adequate instruction and are comfortable with your grip, we will begin with the forehand and backhand strokes, called the ground strokes.

First, the forehand stroke. Use your own variation of the Eastern forehand grip. If you are a right-handed tennis player and the surface in front of backboard has dimensions of regular court, stand halfway inside service line with left side of hip facing backboard, your right foot pointed toward side line and left foot pointed toward backboard. Have your racket back and racket head dropped low. Drop the ball approximately a foot in front of left foot. As you follow through with your forehand stroke, your weight moves forward on your left foot. The left shoulder digs in toward your left foot. Swing your racket up, smash the ball, and finish your stroke with the racket coming up as high as your head.

Morey echoes, "Racket back, weight forward and swing up."

Remember, a backboard never misses a shot. When the ball returns, be ready—racket back, weight forward and swing up. This practice drill is like other exercise programs. Set a goal: start with 25 forehand strokes, without a miss; then 50; then 100; and on up. As you progress, stand further back from the backboard until you reach the service line.

Should you be a left-handed tennis player, turn your right hip toward backboard and follow the same instructions. The other stroke instructions are geared to right-handed tennis players. Follow the same instructions, only gear them to left hand. Remember, racket back low, weight forward and swing up.

Second, the backhand stroke. Adjust your hand to backhand grip. Stand with the right side of your hip facing the backboard, left foot pointed toward the side line, while right foot is pointed toward backboard. Drop ball approximately a foot in front of right foot. As you follow through with the backhand stroke, your weight and shoulder dig in low on your right foot.

Again, Morey echoes, "Racket head back low, weight forward and swing up."

To make backboard practice more interesting, keep a diary—a record of how many strokes you hit without missing your first day. See how much you have improved by the end of each month. You develop your strokes like the JOGGER does. He does not jog five miles the first day unless he is stupid. He builds up to the five miles.

(Above) Volley forehand

(Top, Right) Volley backhand

(Below, Right) Eastern grip for volley

(Below) Service position

Third, the volley or net play. This is fast, fierce action. To understand the volley and master it, will add as much strength to your game as Gatorade does to the exhausted tennis player.

To practice the volley on the backboard, stand approximately 6 feet from backboard. Your racket is held perpendicular to the backboard, with head flat facing the wall. Now, imagine your arm moving in a V toward the backboard. The forehand volley will be the right leg of the V. Push your right arm toward the end of V. The backhand will be the left leg of the V. Never have your racket back, rather, always in front of you, ready to move your arm toward the end of the V. You do not swing your racket on a volley, you tighten your wrist and PUNCH the ball.

The Eastern backhand grip is an excellent grip to use, as you do not have time to change grips during a fast volley.

Start with your forehand volley, remember to *punch* the ball, moving your arm toward the end of the right leg of the V. Do this until you can hit 100 balls without a mistake. When you do, in the background you will hear Morey exclaim, "NOW THAT'S RIGHT."

Next, punch the ball with your backhand volley by moving arm toward the end of the left leg of the V. Do this until you hit the ball 100 times without a mistake.

After you have conquered the forehand volley and the backhand volley, put the two together without letting the ball hit the surface for 100 times or more, without a mistake.

Then set a higher goal for your diary. With this practice, you will become quick and agile. Suddenly, you will realize you are a more aggressive tennis player. A secret ingredient for a sure WINNER.

Remember, volley practice improves your game.

Fourth, the service. To conquer an excellent service may make you "conqueror" of the court.

"Remember," quips Morey, "if you don't get the service in, there is no play."

"No play?" asks a beginner.

"That's right," Morey answers, as he nods his head toward his right shoulder, as though he were adding an exclamation mark.

He advises his students to work on a steady, dependable service, where second serve is as strong as first. He does not advise you to try to develop an ACE, followed by a "sissy pat."

(Top) Height of toss

(Center) How to hold ball for toss

(Bottom) Racket correct position for service

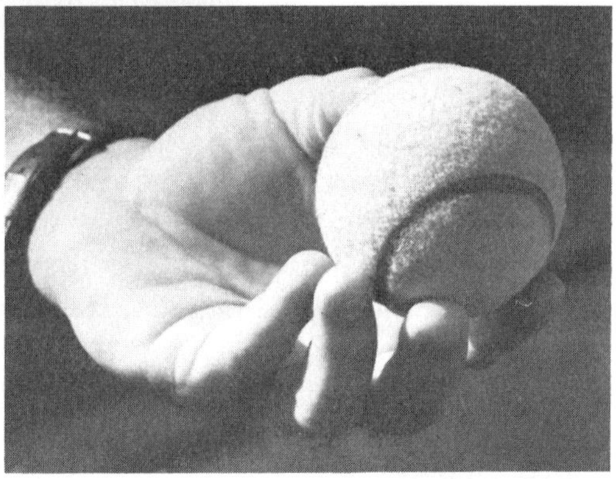

"That's the first sign you aren't a mellowed player," Morey insists.

Now, to begin practice service. First, decide on your grip. Then if backboard's surface is marked with court dimensions, stand behind base line. If surface is not marked, stand 29 feet from backboard. That is the distance you would stand in actual play.

Stand with your feet comfortably separated, slightly angled toward the base line. The backboard should have two circles three feet above the net, one circle for left court service, and one for right court service. This circle is your target.

Hold your racket with your racket head pointed toward your toes. Now you are ready for the important toss.

"Your tennis toss should become your 'closest buddy'," explains Morey, "as the success of your serve depends on it."

First, hold the tennis ball delicately with the tips of your fingers. Do not let the ball touch the palm of your hand. Do not let the ball have a spin on the toss. Imagine your hand as an ice cream cone and the ball an ice cream. If your were going to toss the ice cream out of the cone and catch it, you would toss straight up, Now toss the ball with your left hand straight up and your left eye should view the tossed ball. If you don't smash the tossed ball, it should hit the court surface approximately six inches in front of your left foot.

"Your toss has to BE AT THE RIGHT PLACE AT THE RIGHT TIME," explains Morey.

If your toss goes in front, your right eye will view the ball, you will arch your body, as you swing, and lose control of your service.

The perfect height for the service is to let the toss hang at a height where your racket head would smash the ball.

Now, for your serve. Toss the ball, bring your racket down to your side, then up behind your head where edge of racket could touch your shoulder blade. Keep your elbow up all the time, then hit the ball at its zenith. Follow through with your serve, dropping your racket down across your left side.

Practice serving to left side of court, then right side. Set your goal—up it every day and keep that SOLO TENNIS diary. To add interest and motivation to your backboard practice, challenge a friend to keep a diary. Compare scores at end of month. See who is edging up the fastest.

Smash!

The fifth stroke is the smash. Choose your grip. Most use the Continental, but it is your choice. With the smash, you hold the racket up straight, like the Statue of Liberty (only don't bend arm), extend arm upward, and hit the ball at its highest peak. There are two differences between a smash and a serve. When you smash a ball, you don't toss the ball. It is zooming toward you. Next, you don't bring racket behind the head, *RATHER*, you bring it straight up, extending your arm, then wham the ball and follow through as you would on your service.

To practice a smash, stand behind base line as you would for a serve. Serve the ball, aiming at bottom line of backboard—not the round targets that are three feet above net. The ball will make a fast return on the rise—run in and SMASH it.

Now, let's practice some slick sly shots—the half-volley, the drop shot, and the slice.

First, the half volley. The difference between a volley and a half-volley is the racket is down but not back. The racket head immediately "pushes" the ball as it bounces. You hit the half-volley with half-ground stroke, the racket down but not back. You push the ball with your wrist, not a full stroke. The shot is a defensive shot because you are caught in a position where you can't hit the offensive ground stroke or volley.

To practice the half volley, start the ball with a forehand stroke. Have your racket head dropped toward the ground—push the ball as it bounces. Keep half-volleying, with a goal of 50 forehand half-volleys, then turn and start the backhand half-volley, 50 times without a mistake.

After you have conquered the forehand-backhand half-volley, put the two together and hit forehand-backhand half volleys 50 times without a mistake. Each day, up your goal for your tennis diary. Disciplined practice will develop your confidence with your half-volley shots.

Another sly slick shot is the drop shot. A drop shot is what it says—your racket drops the ball over the net. Your racket head is slightly tilted, and with a little twist of the wrist, flip ball upward, clearing net by a few feet and landing close to net. This shot is MURDEROUS if your opponent is slow and hangs at the base line; however, if he is quick and agile, he may murder you with your drop shot.

When you practice on the backboard, you're getting excellent practice with your timing, keeping eye on ball, and footwork.

"SOLO TENNIS is 'grooming' your game," declares Morey.

Weight forward follow through: Backhand stroke (Top).

Forehand stroke (Bottom).

Another "foxy" shot is the slice.

The slice improves your tennis by suddenly changing the pace of the game. The bounce will startle your opponent, as it is unpredictable. The slice shot is a steady, slow ball; thus a low bounce and less chance of error. Master the slice and your game will be more accurate. You can use the slice and your game will be more accurate. You can use the slice on all basic strokes and the slick sly shots.

"We have gotten so sophisticated, we start kids out hitting flat shots, top spin, everything *but* the slice," Morey claims.

To slice the ball, use a forehand or backhand grip. ONLY slightly angle your racket head—hit down *under* the ball. You may follow through with your forehand-backhand stroke or, if a high bounce, follow through your slice as you would your service.

The angled racket and hitting *under* the ball and following through with your forehand or backhand stroke, is the secret we have that the "non-slicer" doesn't have. Let's keep that secret.

The advantage of a slice shot over a regular ground stroke is the steadiness—makes it easier to keep ball in play—keeps ball low—makes a heavy ball. You don't hit the slice on every ground stroke. It is used to change pace of game.

"Just remember," says Morey, "when in trouble—SLICE."

Don't forget your tennis diary. Set your goal: first, 50 forehand slice shots, then 50 backhand slice shots, then mix in some drop shots. Up your goal each day.

Now your SOLO TENNIS stroke repertoire is forehand, backhand, volley, service and smash, plus the slick sly shots—the half volley, drop shot and slice.

Chapter Four

HOW TO BUILD A TENNIS BACKBOARD

There is a variety of tennis backboards, just as there is a variety of ice cream flavors. Some examples are: wooden walls, brick walls, haydite blocks or concrete walls. The wooden tennis backboard may be the cheapest, but its reputation is the LOUDEST.

The stage sought after in tennis is to develop the strokes and footwork so they flow naturally and not to think of the various techniques of each stroke. "This is what backboard practice develops," states Morey, as he grooves his strokes in front of the tennis backboard.

Usually the tennis backboard is painted green, with a white line 3 feet above the court surface. The United States Lawn Tennis Association's suggestions of tennis backboard dimensions and construction will be discussed later in this chapter.

At the top of some tennis backboards, there is a chicken wire fence or tennis netting to make the wall higher and keep the ball from flying over the backboard. Some have round circles 6 inches above the net line to practice accuracy of service. There are backboards with plastic round disks 6 inches above the net line. If the ball hits the disk, there is a different noise, so there would be no doubt as to whether one hit the disk, should his service be too fast for the eye to see.

Some interesting innovations of the tennis backboard are the side walls of buildings that have paved parking lots in front of the wall. These buildings are used after the working day has ended and the lot is empty, or on Sundays and holidays. Another idea is a closed garage door or doors with a hard-surface driveway of a private home. These innovations don't provide the net, but masking tape could be taped 3 feet from the surface. Then you would be in "tennis business."

The cost of a tennis backboard depends on the kind that is built and prevailing construction costs in various locations. However, the cost for a haydite block tennis backboard is approximately $1,400, and a wooden one is approximately $800, depending on the size and surface used in front of the wall.

"The qualities of a great tennis player are balance, grace, timing and mobility. All of these tennis virtues may be developed with backboard practice," Morey declares.

The United States Lawn Tennis Association has had so many requests from tennis clubs, schools and individuals that it has compiled instructions on how to build a tennis backboard. These suggestions for construction of the tennis backboard from the USLTA are:

General Suggestions For Tennis Practice Board

The advice of a carpenter or contractor should be obtained before constructing a practice board, as local conditions may require some variation of the following:

How To Build a Practice Board

The necessity for a tennis practice board in the development of the various strokes required to round out the game of younger players is so generally recognized by schools, colleges and clubs that the construction of such boards is steadily increasing. In order to meet the numerous requests for data on such construction, the USLTA submits the following general suggestions, as well as specific information offered by several outstanding schools and clubs which have built and have such practice boards in operation at the present time.

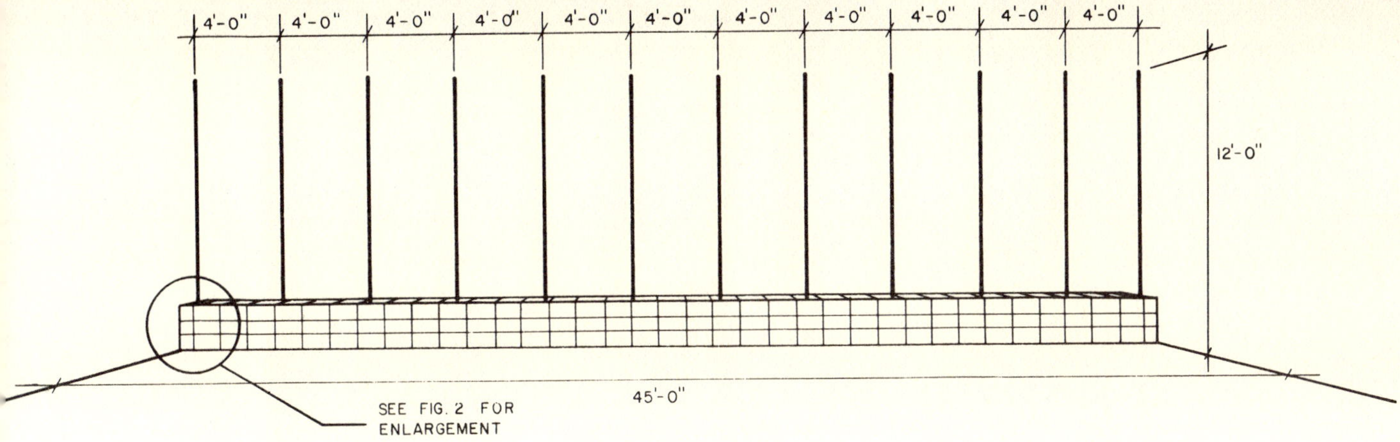

(Above) **FIGURE 1 -- Backboard foundation**

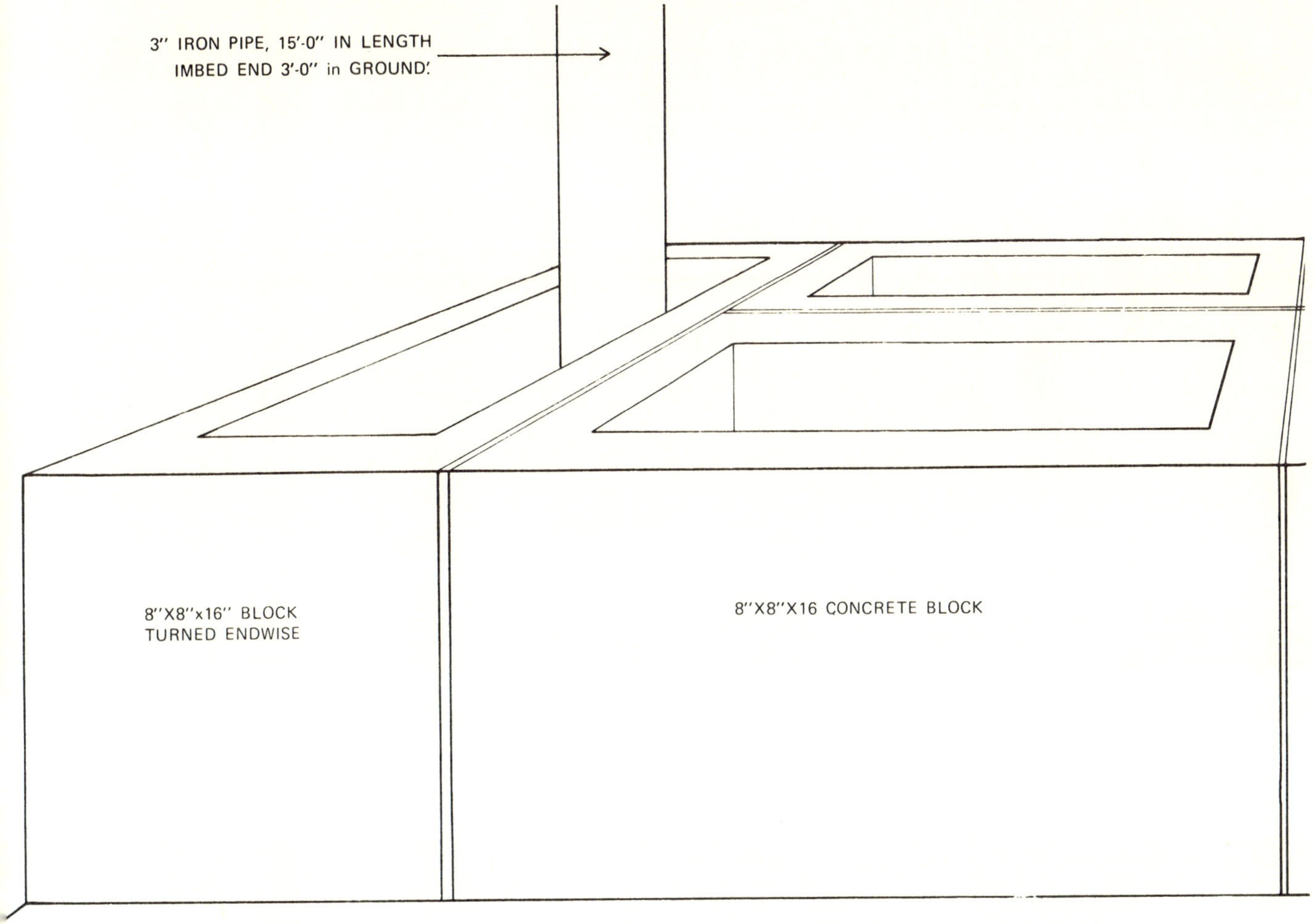

(Above) **FIGURE 2 – Backboard foundation detail** (Below) **FIGURE 3 -- Wire Capping**

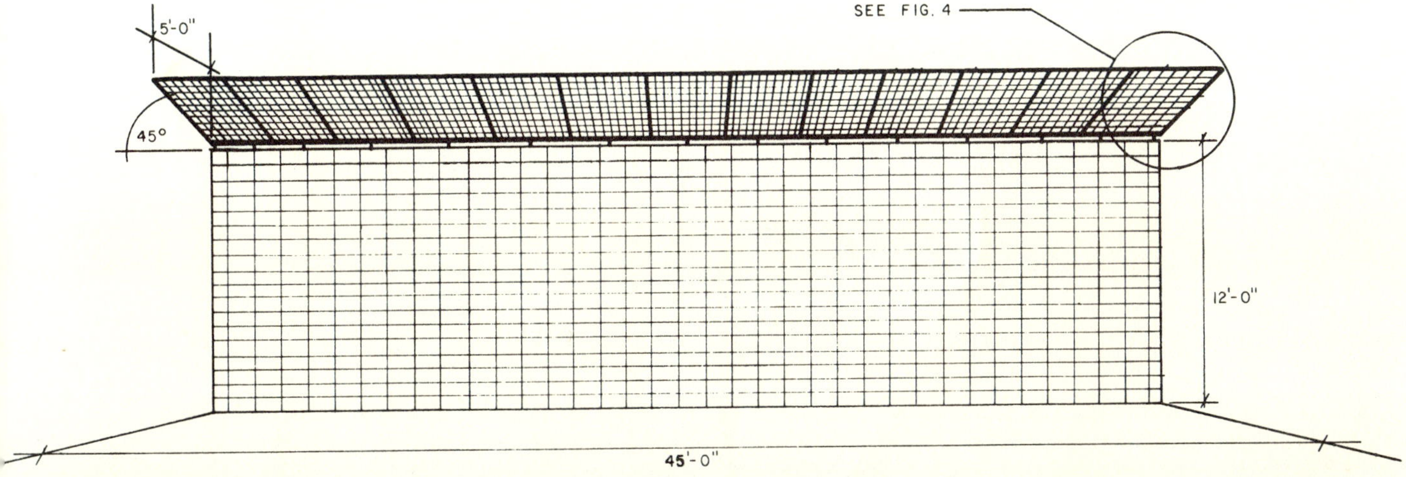

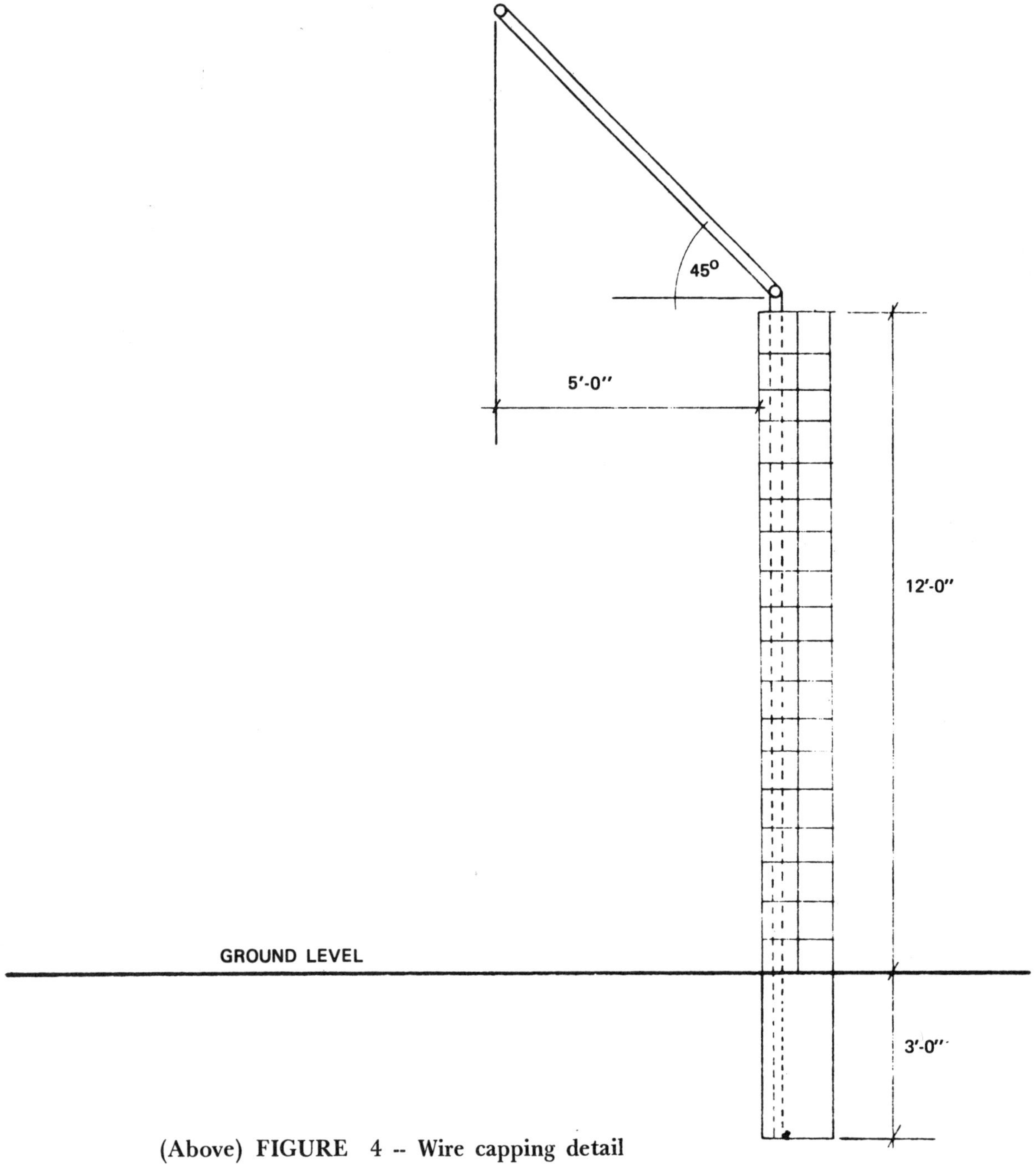

(Above) FIGURE 4 -- Wire capping detail

(Below) FIGURE 5 -- Backboard completed

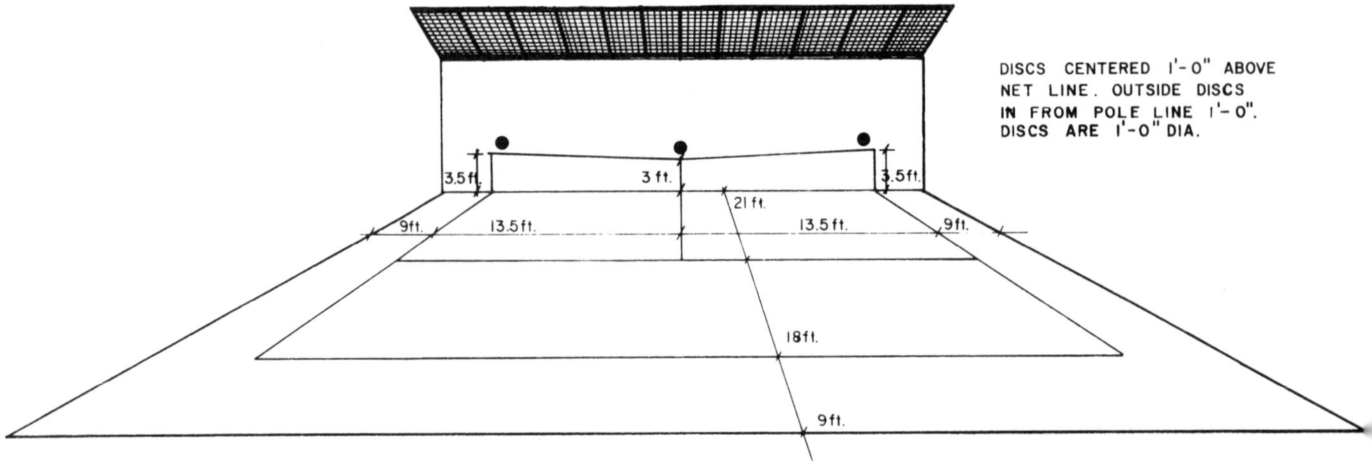

LENGTH

15 to 60 ft. divided into 15 ft. units, if desired, so that more than one player can practice at a time.

HEIGHT

12 ft.

SUPPORTING POSTS

15 ft. vertical 4″ × 4″ posts spaced 5 ft. apart and sunk in 3 ft. of concrete or creosoted and sunk 3 ft. in ground and braced by 2″ × 3″ supports.

HORIZONTAL FURRING

2″ × 2″ furring spaced 1 ft. apart from bottom to top of uprights.

REBOUND SURFACE

2″ tongue and groove finished floor boards, 5″ or 6″ wide and nailed vertically to the cross furring by 4″ galvanized nails, counter-sunk, at least 3 nails to a board.

MARKINGS

Practice board to be painted dark green with a white line indicating proper position of top of net 3 feet above court surface at the center and raising toward the edges. Also, if desired, a horizontal line 11 ft. hight marking "lob" line.

Three or more disks may also be painted 6″ to 12″ above the net line, at positions where the ball should cross the net on a cross-court drive and a drive straight down the lines. These disks or targets are so placed to teach accuracy in driving, since the players try to hit the targets in returning the ball off the board. They are particularly helpful to the more advanced player. (If, instead of disks, holes are cut in the same positions, interest in practice may be increased.)

TOP NET

Support pieces nailed to top of uprights, projecting at an upward angle of about 30 degrees and extending outward over the practice board about 5 ft. to be topped with 1″ chicken wire or old tennis netting.

SCARBOROUGH SCHOOL, SCARBOROUGH-ON-HUDSON, N.Y.— The school practice boards are 10 ft. high and 10 ft. wide. They are made of tongue and groove 2″ flooring lumber mounted on 2″ × 4″'s, and are placed at the back of the court. They are painted battleship gray. The

(Above) Wooden backboard

(Above) Using wall of brick building for backboard

(Below) Large wooden backboard with wire capping

boards are located at the end of a pair of courts off to the side and the other two at the end of a singles court.

BRATTLEBORO (VT.) OUTING CLUB—The club's practice board was built as follows: The framework is made of four 12 ft. × 4″ × 4″ hemlock posts set 6 ft. apart and 3 ft. into the ground. The actual work on the board was done with the whole thing laid flat on the ground. The four posts were laid on the ground first and on top of these were laid five 2″ × 4″'s flat side down and securely spiked on the posts, which makes them parallel to the ground. Every joint was painted before putting the pieces together so as to make the whole thing as weather and waterproof as possible. On top of these was laid (as it lay on the ground) a floor of ordinary 3″ matched fur flooring. Each edge of board was painted also before it was laid so that when the board was finished, there was no joint that was exposed to the elements.

This makes a board which is 18 ft. long and 9 ft. high with the board laid vertical. As the boards run this way, there is no piecing of the floor as the longest piece is only 9 ft. long. The boards were raised into place and secured by using four 2″ × 4″ planks as braces. These were spiked to the top of the braces and then to four 10″ × 10″ posts set 2 ft. into the ground. As this particular board was set against a low bank, there was no need for full-length braces, but where ground is level, longer braces would be needed.

On top of this board is a head piece which makes a sort of roof over the width of the board and forms a drip edge on the back side to prevent the water from running down the full height of the boards.

Above all this is a screen of 2″ × 4″'s which slants out over the front of the board at an angle of about 30 degrees from the perpendicular. The long pieces are 6 ft. long and are extended down to the back side to join the main 2″ × 4″ braces to which they are spiked. The top end is joined by another 2″ × 4″ spiked to the ends of the long pieces. On this frame was originally fastened common poultry wire, but this did not prove at all satisfactory as the force of the balls which hit it soon broke through it in a few days. Inasmuch as the width of the board is half the width of a tennis court, we hung in place of the poultry wire an old net cut in half. One part of this was hung along the extreme outer edge of the frame and the other piece about halfway down the slant of the frame. As these are fastened only at top and on the extreme ends, there is enough "give" to it so that there is not the wear and tear on them that there was on the netting which was stretched taut.

On either side there are wings which extend out for 12 ft. and about 45 degrees. These are of the same construction as the frame on top of the board itself as netting, etc., soon gives way under the constant pounding of the balls.

The whole board is painted a grass green. On this is painted a white line indicating the proper position that the net takes on the court; that is, 3 ft. high at the center and raising towards the edges. The playing surface should, of course, be the same as that on the courts themselves.

HORACE MANN SCHOOL FOR BOYS, NEW YORK, N.Y.—The school's practice board is 12 ft. × 50 ft. in size and of 3″ tongue and groove pine boards laid vertically. No targets of any kind are used other than a painted line indicating the height of the net. A 6ft. high wire screen on top of the wall is valuable for stray hit balls. The concrete floor surface is 50 ft. × 36 ft.

HAVERFORD (PA.) SCHOOL—The specifications of the school's practice board, which has been used with great success, follow: The board is 6 ft. 4″ high and 80 ft. long and extends along an all-weather playcourt. Due to a natural slope in the ground, the board has a different height at one end than at the other to keep it in the proper perspective with its background.

Perhaps the board would be more efficient if three or four feet were added to the top. For experienced players with good sound strokes, the board is high enough; for youngsters starting to play, it is not high enough and very often they hit over the board.

THE PRACTICE BOARD

Indispensable for Beginners and Helpful to Advanced Players

The marked improvement in forehand and backhand drives resulting from frequent use of the practice board is becoming more generally appreciated by progressive schools and clubs which have installed them. The very obvious advantages of a practice board are that the player can get excellent practice by himself in overcoming the particular weakness which requires attention and, secondly, the instructor can stand beside the player and watch every detail of the stroke much more closely than if he were stationed 40 or 50 feet away on the opposite side of the net. At close range it is easy to teach basic essentials—balance, shifting of weight from rear to front foot, swing, timing, position of racket at time of impact, follow-through. When once these fundamentals have been learned, the player has a sound foundation upon which a real game can be built in practice on the court and in competition. Even the expert tournament player finds the practice board invaluable in providing a definite way to overcome his weaknesses.

At the start, the young player should be stationed a short distance from the practice board, five or six feet, and shown by the instructor HOW TO HIT THE BALL RATHER SOFTLY AGAINST THE BOARD AND RETURN IT WITH AN EVEN SWING. The player should be particularly warned against crowding the ball, a habit which nearly all beginners and young players adopt and which must be corrected by careful and patient instruction. He should be taught not to hit the ball too close to the body, which cramps his stroke. Gradually the distance from the board should be increased, the player instructed to hit the ball harder, and with a low trajectory. At this point, the follow-through, body balance, and the shifting of the weight from the rear foot to the front foot on forehand and backhand drives should be taught, together with frequent advice to focus the eyes on the ball.

The practice board should be as wide as a singles court, if space permits, with a painted line across the board to represent the height of the net. Three or more disks should be painted 6″ above the net line, at positions where the ball should cross the net on a cross-court drive and a drive straight down the line. These disks or targets are so placed to teach accuracy in driving, since the players try to hit the targets in returning the ball off the board. They are particularly helpful to the more advanced player.

There are games played on the tennis backboard. As an example, the player can march to the backboard to play "Solo Tennis." How? Don't forget your tennis diary. Set your own goals. If you want your goal for a particular day to be 25 forehands without a miss, then 25 backhands without a miss, then cross court, set your own combination. Let your

(Above) Students practicing on backboard

(Below) Regular court surface in front of backboard

(Below) Using garage doors as backboard

competitive disposition compete with yourself. The next time you go to play "Solo Tennis," beat your last record—be a WINNER! At the same time you are grooving your strokes.

Too, you can play the "Wall Game." It is played just like tennis, only it is played at the tennis backboard. First, two players spin their racket for service as you would in regular tennis. Then the server stands behind the base line as he does in tennis. His opponent stands in opposite court as he would for net play. The server serves the ball. If he hits the service mark above the net line and his opponent does not return the ball—the score is 15-love—the server's score comes first like tennis. However, should the receiver return the ball, the players alternate turns, keeping ball in play as long as possible until a player is forced into making an error, giving the point to the other player. Should the server miss the service mark, he may have another serve. Should he miss the mark again, the point goes to his opponent. No let balls in "Wall Game."

The "Wall Game" is played in sets, as in tennis. The first player winning 7 games with a two game lead wins the set. Should there be a 7-7 tie, they would go into a five point tie breaker. The player who did *not* start the set with the first service starts the five point tie breaker by serving first. He serves the first point, then the service is alternated after each player has served two points. The player who wins five points first wins the game.

Should the tennis backboard not have a court surface in front of the backboard, the two players spin for service, then alternate hitting the backboard's return. The player who misses the backboard's return loses the point.

The "Wall Game" is played all over the country—especially when the courts are full and there is "waiting time." Don't wait in a chair—PRACTICE by playing the "Wall Game" or play SOLO TENNIS.

Footwork for service return

Chapter Five

DEVELOPING FORM ON TENNIS BACKBOARD

"In tennis, your 'ace in the hole' is proper footwork," declares Morey.

Actually, proper footwork is the secret ingredient in many events, such as dancing, boxing and football. However, the tennis backboard is excellent for developing proper footwork in the game of tennis. With enough practice, the player will automatically step in the right direction, just as automatic as keeping the racket back for ground strokes. "When proper footwork becomes automatic—start dusting off your trophy shelf," warns Morey. As an example, he points to Jimmy Connors as the world's champion because of his excellent footwork.

Footwork and timing are like twins, in that footwork is balance and control, while timing is transferring weight to the right foot before striking the ball. When these twins are mastered, you will "master" your opponent.

There are four basic requisites to accomplish proper footwork. They are: (1) spin on heels of your feet to right position for service return; (2) be alert and ready to slice or glide to ball; (3) half-step for close shots instead of running; and (4) step the left foot across the right foot toward the right alley for forehand, and step the right foot across the left foot toward left alley for the backhand. These four basic rules for proper footwork can be practiced on the backboard. For the first rule, stand at the service line or approximately 39 feet from the backboard. Now stand as you would to return a service, then spin your heels to the right for a forehand return—bring your left foot across your right foot—drop the ball out in front of you—follow through with a forehand stroke. As the ball hits the backboard and bounces back, catch it and repeat. Exchange footwork to left and follow the same instructions for backhand service return.

The second requisite may be practiced by standing in front of backboard—alert to slide or glide between the practiced strokes.

To practice the third rule, stand with hip and toes pointing to the right alley for a forehand stroke. Drop the ball and hit it so the ball will bounce close to you and half-step to stroke it. Repeat for backhand, only turn hip and toes toward left alley.

The fourth rule for proper footwork can be practiced on the backboard by practicing your forehand and backhand strokes. That is the footwork you use on those strokes.

Don't forget to keep your tennis diary and "up" your goal each day. If you do, you will "up" your tennis ladder, too.

Akin to the tennis footwork is the tennis stance, or the relative position of the player's feet and ball when making a stroke. The stance allows the player to shift his weight into the ball. There are three different stances. They are the closed stance, semi-closed stance, and the open stance.

For the closed stance, the player stands facing the backboard, pivots his right heel toward the right alley, while partially crossing the left foot in front of the right foot. His left hip automatically faces the net. He is now ready to follow through with his forehand stroke. For the backhand closed stance footwork, the player pivots the left heel toward the left alley and follows the same instruction for forehand closed stance footwork.

The disadvantages of the closed stance are as follows. First, the player has a tendency to go sideways into the ball instead of going forward. Next, the player's body is in the way and usually causes him to have only one choice for his shot—down the line.

With semi-closed stance, the left foot does not cross the right foot as much, nor does the right foot cross the left foot as much. This way, the weight can be transferred to left or right foot much easier. "Your body is not in the way and the ball can be hit down the line or cross court," explains Lance Dryer, who is a young pro who works with Morey.

The third stance is the open stance, used mainly by advanced players. "Bjorn Borg's open stance is the best example of an advanced player," states Morey.

The open stance gives more of a disguise for the player's return shot. The player stands facing the net, with the left foot pulled slightly back. Its disadvantage is if player doesn't know proper footwork, he can get sloppy

These three stances may be practiced on the tennis backboard by the "one ball" practice.

To practice the closed stance, the player stands approximately 15 feet in front of backboard facing it. Next, he pivots his right heel so right foot is slightly facing the right alley. Then he partially crosses the right foot with his left foot, turning his left hip sideways to the net. Then he drops "one" ball in front of racket and follows through with forehand stroke, catching the ball off the bounce and repeats. This is the same practice for the service, only the player is not standing as far from the backboard. The player pivots his heels to left alley for backhand open stance footwork.

The semi-stance is practiced for forehand and backhand, the same way as closed stance—only don't cross the feet as much as picture indicates.

To practice the open stance, the player stands 15 or 20 feet from backboard with his toes pointing toward the wall, his legs comfortably separated. Then the same "one ball" method. He drops the ball—follows through with his forehand or backhand stroke. He catches the ball off the bounce and repeats as many times as he desires.

Remember, "Open stance for advanced player only."

Another "key to successful tennis" is keeping the eye on the ball. Morey says, "There is no excuse for a 'shifty-eyed' tennis player."

The court surface is not fickle—it won't change. The alley will be where the alley always is—true for the service line and back court line. So the trained tennis eye follows the ball constantly, rather than gazing at the court or an opponent.

"Backboard practice is excellent to develop the habit of keeping your eye on the ball," Morey declares.

Concentration separates the men from the boys in most any game, especially in tennis. "A player can't go to the tennis backboard and practice any tennis mechanics without exercising CONCENTRATION," says Morey. This habit is easily transferred to actual play on the tennis court, as is the habit of being in ready position with racket back.

(Left) Closed stance
(Top, Right) Semi backhand closed stance
(Bottom, Right) Open stance
(Below, Left) Semi forehand closed stance

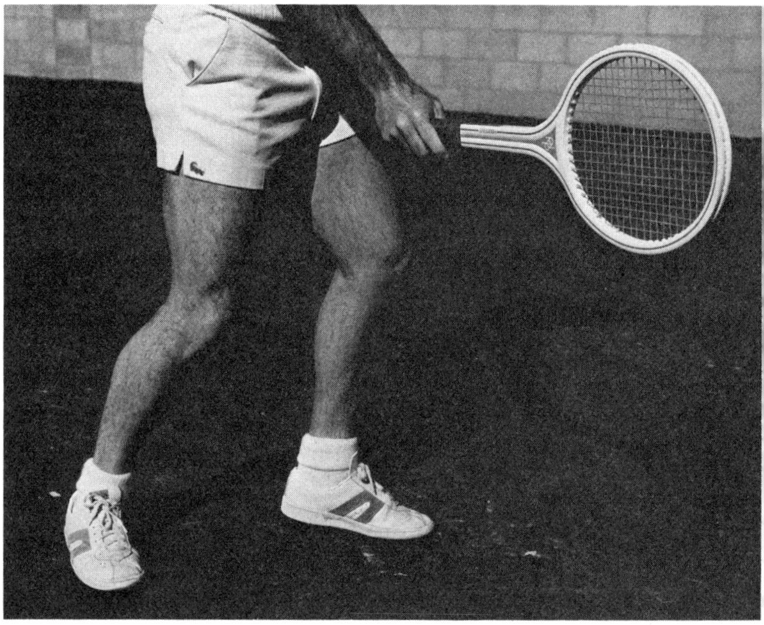

Chapter Six

CORRECTING BAD HABITS ON TENNIS BACKBOARD

''A player's bad habits on the tennis court can easily be spotted—they are as obvious as bad table manners,'' says Morey. ''And he had better do something about them,'' he quickly adds.

When a player's game is off, he can spot his own weaknesses and can march to the tennis backboard and groove his bad habits away. ''However,'' Morey advises, ''if he has any doubt about WHY he is making so many errors on the court, he should take his Pro to the backboard with him, for he may use the backboard to continue his bad habits rather than correct them.''

Taking a Pro to the backboard occasionally is stretching your ''tennis teaching'' money. As an example, a Pro can stand at the player's side at the backboard and be in a better position to see the player's strokes, footwork, stance and other tennis techniques. When the Pro is standing across the net, he can't see EVERYTHING and can't be as quick to point out the player's bad habits.

The most common errors or bad habits the player develops are: hurrying the ball, rushing the ball, not following through with his stroke, timing, overhead smash, keeping the eye on the ball, and service.

Let's examine these bad habits.

If a player finds he flubs his shot and the ball darts cross court—only on *his* side of the net, he obviously lacks accuracy. This is what hurrying a ball causes. Usually a player hits the ball too early and hurries his stroke because he is not a good tennis Boy Scout. He forgot to—BE PREPARED. When a player hurries his stroke, he will hit the ball too far in front of him and the uncontrolled ball will zoom too far to the right or left.

"The way to avoid hurrying the ball," explains Morey, "is to be alert—make the decision before the ball crosses the net—whether to be ready for backhand or forehand stroke—take your time—exercise the stroke smooth and exact."

If a player hurries his stroke, he will add another bad habit—he will flip his wrist or snap at the ball. This takes away the possibility of developing a graceful stroke.

Next, over-running the ball. Anxiety quietly boils up in a player in a tight tennis match. This can make a player too eager and he will over-run a ball. When a player over-runs a ball, he cramps his stroke and makes a smooth, swift stroke impossible. If a player over-runs the ball, he is in bad trouble. If this bad habit develops, cool off on the inside—take your time—stay out of trouble.

If a player does not follow through on his ground strokes, it will cause the ball to fly out of the court, or smash into the net. If most of a player's balls are taking this course, he knows he has a bad habit that he must correct.

A checklist for this bad habit is as follows: The player should check to see if his body is sideways to the net—if his racket is back and low—if his weight flows forward—if his eyes see the ball contact the racket—if the racket ends up at least shoulder high. If a player isn't using all of these techniques, he needs to polish his ground strokes on the tennis backboard.

"When a player does not follow through with his strokes, he will become a jerky tennis player," says Morey.

READY—AIM—FIRE! That's timing. Should this command be given to a group and one or two did not fire at the exact time, the effect would be lost.

If a player is not hitting the ball in front of him, but hitting the ball behind him, his timing is off. His effect will be lost. "If your timing is off, your game will be off," says Morey.

Timing overshadows a player's game. Exact timing is needed for his service, ground strokes, footwork, and volley shots. It's the tennis key to start the game.

A player who is having trouble with his timing may need to correct this bad habit by getting prepared early for every tennis technique.

"My game was off today," is an all too common complaint among tennis players. The player knows his good days and his bad days. Usually his bad days are caused by "poor timing."

What causes this poor timing? Many times it is because the player is not in good physical or mental shape. In some cases the player may have been off the courts for several days or weeks, and lost his timing from lack of practice.

"Timing comes from hitting lots of balls," explains Morey.

Next, if a player is playing before a gallery and he misses a spectacular overhead smash, he will hear a groaning gallery. If he lacks a gallery, he will hear himself groan.

"This bad habit of missing an overhead SMASH is caused by lack of concentration and timing," adds Morey.

It is important to master this stroke. If executed correctly, it's a sure WINNER. Also, it is the answer to the devastating pace-changing lob.

The mechanics of the overhead smash are those of the service.

If a player is having trouble with his smash, his checklist should be: his position, his grip, his hips sideways, his racket in back-scratching position. If the player has to check many of these techniques, he had better "check in" at the tennis backboard.

Let's examine the service.

If a player develops an accurate zooming serve, his opponent will fear him as much as he would a cornered rattlesnake.

The weak points in a serve are toss—not letting any movement of an opponent or anything else disturb his concentration; and a "pitty pat" second serve—not starting toss and backswing at the same time.

"Work HARD on any of these weak points," demands Morey.

Now to the tennis backboard to give these bad habits a workout.

First, hurrying the stroke. The player should stand approximately 12 or 15 feet in front of the backboard, in the position for a forehand or backhand stroke. Have racket back, drop the ball in front of left foot, hit the ball and count three before hitting the ball. Begin with a slow pace and stroke as many balls as necessary, until the player has developed the right feel for a smooth stroke. "If the player practices this enough, he won't ever rush his stroke," declares Morey.

To practice not over-running the ball, the player strokes the ball against the backboard, doublechecking position of his feet, racket and shoulders. Correct position will erase this bad habit, because if the player is correctly prepared early for his shot, he will not over-run the ball.

If the player is not following through with his strokes, causing "wild" balls, he should stand 15 or 20 feet from the backboard in position for the forehand stroke and hit the ball 25 times without missing the ball. Have the racket back, drop the ball slightly in front of the left foot, hit the ball and let racket follow through, ending at least shoulder high. Continue this forehand stroke until the ball has been smoothly hit for at least 25 times without a miss. Then practice the backhand stroke the same way, hitting the ball 25 times without a miss—then "up" the tennis diary and stroke 50 forehand and backhand strokes without a miss.

If a player's bad habit is timing, Morey says, "Go to the backboard and hit lots of balls with the various strokes, and your timing will become automatic."

Should missing the overhead smash be the player's weakness, backboard practice will "smash" this weakness, backboard practice will "smash" this weakness away. Stand slightly behind the service line in position for a serve. Toss the ball as you would for a serve and hit the ball downward, approximately 6 inches in front of the backboard. The ball will climb up the wall and bounce back as a high lob. Follow the tennis techniques previously given for the overhead smash.

Finally, strengthening a weak serve. The player should stand approximately 39 feet from backboard or behind the service line. Stand in proper position for the serve. If a player's toss is causing his service weakness, place a tin can lid slightly in front of the forward toe. Toss the ball at your established height and in front of your right eye. Practice tossing the ball and letting it hit the tin lid.

When the player feels he has practiced his toss enough to have control of it, then he should start serving the ball, aiming at the white circle or disk that is 6 inches above the net line. Serve the ball, catch it, and repeat until the player has conquered a "hero" serve.

Don't forget stretching your tennis teaching money by occasionally taking a Pro to the backboard with you. "You can develop bad habits *practicing* on the backboard if you don't concentrate on every tennis technique and do them right," Morey wisely advises.

(Left) Hurrying the ball

(Below) Not following through with stroke

(Right) Not keeping eye on ball

(Above) Missing over head smash

(Right) Poor service position

(Below) Foot Fault

Chapter Seven

HOW TO SHARPEN YOUR TENNIS INTELLIGENCE

"Don't be a sassy smart aleck on the tennis court—be SMART—develop your tennis IQ," Morey advises his players.

Tennis is not only a game of muscle flexing and physical stamina, it is a quick-thinking, outsmarting-your-opponent game.

Some "tennis IQ" tips are: Court position. A player can pull his opponent off the court with a wide serve. When his opponent runs off court to return the ball, the other half of the court is wide open. An open court to a fast-thinking tennis player is as deadly as poison. A fast cross court return of an opponent's serve will draw him off court, too. Another way to topple an opponent's court position is to draw him to net with a drop shot, then lob over him. "Remember, pulling an opponent out of position is SMART TENNIS," Morey reminds his students.

A player can practice the execution of drawing his opponent off court by practicing his service, cross court return and drop shot at the tennis backboard.

"Mexico's champion, Ramirez, is one of the best examples of concentrating on pulling an opponent off court," says Morey. "Next time you see Ramirez in a tennis match on TV, watch him do this. Then you can see smart style tennis," he adds.

To play smart tennis you have to make quick decisions—decisions like which stroke—backhand, forehand; where to return the ball; the opponent's court position. These smart, quick decisions are as important to a player as accurate, graceful strokes and quick, agile footwork. If a player's brains are either weak or lazy, he has a bad handicap to begin with. In tennis, it's "oursmart" or "be outsmarted."

"Another good 'tennis IQ' tip is for the tennis player to develop a full game," Morey advises. A SMART tennis player will round out his game. So the first "goal" of a serious tennis player should be to work on an "all weather" game. Good volley, good baseline, good cross court returns, good service—and GOOD tennis is sure to follow.

A *smart* player needs to consider the "percentage shot." "A percentage shot is a shot that gives the player the advantage of making the shot a winner," explains Morey. The basic rule for the percentage shot is to get the ball back or your service in. "Now that's the GOLDEN RULE in tennis—you had better believe it," Morey warns, as he nods his head affirmatively.

Once the ball is in play, an example of a percentage shot is hitting the ball down the side line when a player is in the opposite court. Cross court shot is a good percentage shot because the net is lower in the middle, and cross court is a longer shot. Still another excellent percentage shot is the lob, whether it is a defensive lob to give the player time to get in court position, or an attacking lob to drive the opponent away from the net. "When in TROUBLE—lob," affirms Morey.

One of the best percentage shots is a player's weakness. This weakness can be spotted while a player is warming up with his opponent. To spot his weakness, the player should mix up his shot repertoire. Give his opponent a fast cross court—see if he recovers his court position quick enough for the next ball. Notice his strokes—see which is the weakest—his backhand stroke or his forehand stroke. If one is weaker, play to that weakness. Then try a drop shot and follow with a lob to see how fast he is. "Watch him watch you, 'cause you'll know what to expect from him," Morey advises.

The warmup with the player's opponent is *important.* It should allow a player to spot his opponent's weakness while he increases the proficiency of his shots.

Still another good percentage shot is to slam the ball at his opponent's feet. This is one of the hardest shots to return, as it tears up grooving a stroke.

Now remember, the good percentage shots are: down the line, cross court, play to an opponent's weakness, and a lob. The bad percentage shots give the *opponent* the advantage of making the shot a winner. Examples are: playing to the opponent's strong stroke, placing ball so opponent can kill it with a smash, the drop shot (particularly if the opponent is speedy), half volley, and lob volley. A lob volley is vollying a ball over the opponent's head instead of swooping the ball high with a full ground stroke.

Remember, percentage shots are part of tennis math. More tennis math is following the flight of ball and getting back to center base line where the player can cover anything his opponent hits. "Master tennis math, and you will be an intelligent player," claims Morey. "A sure WINNER," he quickly adds.

Just as the basic traits of a gentleman are good manners, a potential tennis winner will have traits than can be spotted. "I watch all my students and have found that the one who works the hardest, practices on the backboard, takes his tennis seriously, plays in tournaments and has a high 'tennis IQ' will be a WINNER," Morey claims.

A winner wants to win. A winner knows he can win. A winner practices to win. A winner never gives a point away. The player who has common sense—an innate desire to win—keeps the ball in play—forces his opponent to err—will drink from the tennis cup of success. "It's that simple," states Morey.

If two players are well matched in their tennis techniques, STRATEGY will tip the winning scales.

Strategy is a many-splendored thing. It is like a backgammon player deciding on playing a Running game, a Blocking game, or a Back game. Decisions have to be made, and made fast—right decisions that give his opponent the feeling he is playing with a tennis authority.

A checklist for tennis strategy is: (1) Placing shots. A player should be patient—wait for an open court to put the ball away. "Placing the shot is more important than pacing the shot," Morey declares. (2) Get in right court position for opponent's return. (3) Mix your game up. SURPRISE your opponent. If you have been sending fast, steady bullet shots, pop an easy one. It throws his timing off and often produces an error from the player's opponent. (4) If the opponent is basically a base line player, that is a clue he is not a good net man. If you are, draw him to net with a short shot and knock him out with a volley punch! (5) ATTACK OR NOT ATTACK—that is the player's decision. If an opponent is attacking and is winning the game, then attack. (6) Go into a match with a plan. Learn as much as you can about an opponent before the match, such as his tennis ability, temperament, physical stamina, and how high is his "tennis IQ." "Remember, the more you know about a subject, the more likely you will pass the test," reminds Morey.

Now to be a tennis "general," every shot the player makes should be thought out. He is in BATTLE with his opponent to kill—not to be killed. The player needs to decide where to place the ball, why he should place the ball where he wants to, whether to draw the opponent off court, whether to bring him to the net or get him used to a certain rhythm, then change pace. "every shot should be thought through and *never* just returned," states Morey.

Strategy in both singles and doubles is making quick decisions and getting in control of game before an opponent does. This is done either attacking or maneuvering your opponent all over the court, or playing a defensive baseline game. Decide which strategy to use and use it!

Remember, a true strategy tennis artist uses the court surface for his canvas, his racket for his brush, and his "shots" for his color. As he strokes his canvas with his strategy shots, he will heavily color the center line and side lines. His quick, fast passing shots will add interest to his "art."

Chapter Eight

PHYSICAL FITNESS AND AGILITY

Tennis luck?

There are few tennis dice that roll seven or eleven on the tennis courts. Occasionally a tennis ball will climb the white tape on top of the net and fall "luckily" on your opponent's court. However, a true tennis player places his balls on the edge of the court's lines, because he has worked hard physically and mentally. He knows "how and where" to stroke the tennis ball for a winner. He can do this because he is physically fit.

Just what is physical fitness? Dr. Kenneth H. Cooper, founder of the Aerobic exercise for the United States Air Force, is now a world renowned expert on physical fitness. His definition of physical fitness is, "Having the strength, endurance, and cardiac reserves necessary to function safely and effectively during all types of physical and emotional stress." Dr. Cooper says when he lectures on physical fitness, he is often asked, "Fit for what?" He answers, "Fit for life."

Dr. Cooper founded the Cooper Clinic in Dallas, Texas. After his clinic has given his patients an extensive physical, he puts them on a physical fitness program.

Each patient is to earn so many points per week in one or more of his suggested Aerobic sports. Tennis is one of his chosen Aerobic sports. Dr.

Cooper claims, "It takes seven hours singles tennis minimum per week to get the Aerobic benefit that is necessary."

Morey quickly adds, "Don't forget that 15 minutes of serious 'Solo Tennis' is equal to one hour of tennis play."

Nevertheless, there is no physical fitness thermometer. However, in doctors' offices there are treadmills to judge one's stamina; pulse readings to judge the pace of one's heartbeat; and instruments to check one's blood pressure.

"A serious tennis player should be under the supervision of a doctor, formulate his exercise program and let it become a regular part of his life," Morey advises.

This means a tennis player must discipline himself into a systematic exercise program. A steady, regular rhythm in any art is better than a sporadic exercise episode. Top tennis play is an acrobatic art.

"Now don't wake up one morning and jog, ride a bicycle and jump a rope, then 'dash' to the tennis court—cause you'll sure get FIRST AID on the court," Morey chuckles.

There are alleys for a tennis player to obtain the height of his physical endurance. "When a player is in "match play" with a trophy or money dangling in front of him, his physical stamina could be the determining factor. A player can't play strong tennis for two or three hours without being in TOP phsical shape. That's how long some of your championship matches last," Morey states.

The first alley to one's top physical endurance is the systematic form of exercise a player decides to participate in.

"This is a good place to use your tennis diary. Watch your stamina increase," reminds Morey. However, TAKE YOUR DOCTOR's ADVICE. If you decide to jog, start with the goal your doctor suggests, then slowly increase the goal to the advised distance and timing. If you walk—do the same. If you skip rope—do the same.

Lance Dryer, Morey's assistant and righthand man, says, "Different exercise help different muscles." Jogging and walking strengthen the legs. Squeezing a rubber ball strengthens the wrist. Sit-ups strengthen the stomach muscles and leg muscles. Chinning a bar strengthens the arms.

Then for the tried true and blue athlete Lance says, "There are exercises such as the double knee jump, the star jump and the L-sit." The Australians made these exercises popular.

(Top) Sitting on tiptoes for leg muscles and physical agility

(Center) Star jump

(Bottom) Double knee jump

(Above) Bringing elbows to knees
(Below) Touching elbows to knees
with heels on concrete

(Opposite page, Top) Beginning of push up
(Opposite page, Center) Push up
(Opposite page, Bottom) The L - Sit

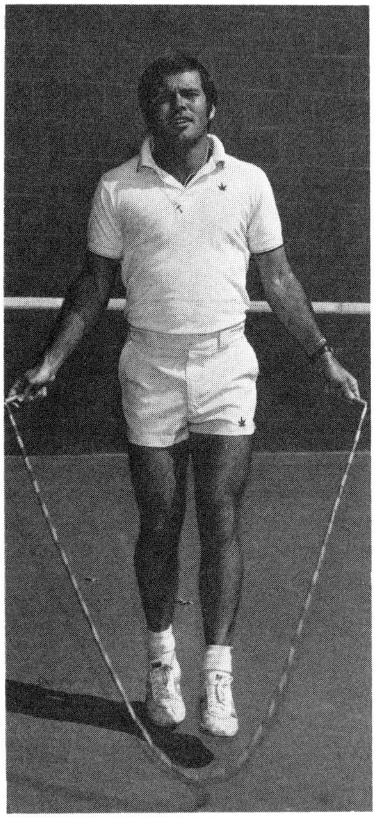

(Left) Skipping Rope

(Center) Jogging around tennis court

(Bottom) Unwinding after jogging

To do the double knee jump, stand on your toes with your feet close together and your arms and hands flat to your side. Then jump as high as you can, bringing your knees up to your chest while your arms embrace your knees. Do this as many times as you can in succession. This exercise develops the "overall" muscles.

To do the star jump, stand on your toes with your feet close together, your hands and arms flat to your side. Then jump as high as you can while stretching your legs as far apart as you can and raising your arms above your head as high as you can. Your two pointed legs, two pointed arms, and your head make five points—thus the STAR jump.

Next the L-sit. Sit on the ground or floor with your legs close together and stretching straight out. Place your arms to the side of your body with your hands open flat on the surface, pointing away from your body—*not* to your feet. Then lift your body straight up off the ground, keeping your back straight and your legs straight and stiff, making an L—thus the L-sit exercise. "That takes care of lots of muscles," Lance insists.

However, don't forget that the double knee jump, star jump, and L-sit exercises are strictly for the "tried true and blue" athletes.

But the serious tennis player, on a scheduled exercise program, should "unwind" after his exercise. That means after his most strenuous exercise, he should exercise in low gear. "As an example," states Lance, "after jogging around the tracks, a player could walk fast on his tiptoes—this tightens the calf muscles in his legs." Too, Lance mixes his unwinding exercises. He walks on his tiptoes—turns, walks backward, then seasons his wind-downs with side skips, like a basketball player does. "Mixing it up cuts the ribbon of boredom," declares Lance.

On the tennis court surface, dimensions are small compared to football, basketball or baseball fields. Tennis demands FAST action. You cover a few yards, but you must be as quick and agile as a flea—running, jumping, stopping, scooping and punching.

"So be sure your exercise program doesn't include plodding or shuffling, but rather dashing and darting," advises Lance.

Another alley to one's top physical endurance is the nutritional alley. Nobody's body is the same, and neither should their diet be the same. However, the body's proper weight in relation to one's height always adds a "plus" factor to good health. So one player may find a certain combination of foods keeps his weight low, while another may find a different combination for his body chemicals.

Nevertheless, proper nutrition is a "must" for physical endurance. This may be supplemented by a daily intake of vitamins recommended by a physician. Now ther is a definite tennis NO-NO under the heading of nutrition. That is *no* alcoholic beverages before tennis play nor during tennis play. Alcohol blurs your vision, blurs your timing, and blurs your stability.

"Before a tennis match, eat sensibly," states Morey. "An overdose of food makes a player sluggish and an underdose will make a player shaky," he explains.

When a player steps on the tennis court to display his physical endurance, he should have a first aid kit in his tennis bag. The first aid kit should have water (no pops), salt tablets, bandaids, and a handy piece of candy for a slug of energy.

Another physical endurance alley is practice. "Practice makes perfect—TENNIS BACKBOARD PRACTICE. Remember, fifteen minutes' backboard practice is equal to approximately an hour of actual play," Morey declares.

Behind the records of any champion in any sport—whether it be skiing, swimming, or scuba diving—are records of hard sacrifices and practice. Should a beginning player with a zeal to reach the champions' mountaintop ask many champions the question, "What is the secret to your success?", their answers would be the same. "Hard work and practice," they would echo.

The same echo of success that has been echoing down the halls of time for centuries—PRACTICE.

Chapter Nine

JUNIOR TENNIS TOURNAMENTS AND SCHOLARSHIPS

"The Junior players of 'today' are the college champions of 'tomorrow' and the professional champions of 'the day after tomorrow,'" Morey professes.

However, if a Junior player is serious about his tennis future, he, or she, will find it a LONELY, HARD journey. Lonely, because a player has to cut strings from other interests and give *all* his free time to tennis.

Most of the better Junior players start at an early age, sometimes as young as eight or nine. They start playing in tournaments at this age. The top Junior players work hard. They work alone on their serve—they work at hitting the service spots on the backboards—they practice grooving their strokes on the backboard—they practice on the courts with other players and they play in tournaments to become "tournament tough."

This lonely, hard tennis journey will get the player his ranking. A player's ranking is based on his yearly sanctioned tournament records. The USLTA ranking committee will look at a Junior player's wins, competitive scores, and losses. They will look for a long, steady record rather than a short record with comparable wins and losses. "This ranking committee wants a player exposed to top quality opponents. So it's WHO you win over or lose to that counts," Morey states.

However, this difficult tennis tournament journey can be rewarding.

A player travels to different sections of his state or nation. He meets many new people and makes many *lifelong* friends. "Don't forget there is a tournament ladder. The better a player becomes, the faster he moves up to the harder tournaments that will raise his ranking," Morey advises his students.

The Junior players in the national tournaments are the top Juniors from the various USLTA sections. These players are endorsed by the sectional endorser—both boys and girls.

However, should a player not be endorsed as one of the top Juniors, he or she can apply to the sectional endorser as an alternate. This means that should the endorsed player be unable to make the tournament, the alternate would play, giving the alternate a chance to "up" his or her ranking.

The endorsed players may play doubles and singles in the tournament. "If a player is going to travel far to a tournament, he should enter doubles *and* singles. Play as much tournament tennis as you can," Morey highly suggests.

Those who are eligible for Junior tennis are:
Boys' 18 refers to 18 and under boys.
Girls' 18 refers to 18 and under girls.
Boys' 16 refers to 16 and under boys.
Girls' 16 refers to 16 and under girls.
Boys' 14 refers to 14 and under boys.
Girls' 14 refers to 14 and under girls.
Boys' 12 refers to 12 and under boys.
Girls' 12 refers to 12 and under girls.

These Junior Boys' and Girls' events shall be open to players in these divisions for the following twelve months who have not reached the highest age limit in these categories before October 1st. As an example, a player who becomes 16 in October or after is eligible to play another full season in the 16 and under division, but a player becoming 16 in September is not eligible for another season in the 16's.

"Remember, tennis is a GENTLEMAN'S game. In Junior tournaments, the player's word is honored—if he ever deliberately lies and is caught, his ranking is crushed because of conduct," warns Morey.

As in other tournaments, the Junior tournaments have different kinds of court surfaces. "The kind of surface will depend on the 'kind' of tennis the player will play,'' asserts Morey. There are as many different kinds of court surfaces and see how it affects tennis strategy.

First, the clay court. There are more clay courts in the tennis world than any other court surface. Even though the maintenance is high, they are easier to build. The clay court surface is the least expensive to construct.

Now most clay courts have a surface dressing that is put on top of the clay base, such as Har-Tru. This porous dressing will cause quick drainage. A dressing may add color—green or red—to the clay surface.

The clay court surface makes the ball bounce higher—thus easier to return. The strategy will be a slower-paced, patient game. Most of the play will be from the base line rather then a vigorous volley at the net. ''The clay court develops a base line game, teaches the player to keep the ball in play, allows lobs, and stresses quick court position,'' says Morey. He adds quickly, ''Like Chris Evert and Manuel Orantes STYLE.''

Another surface is the grass court. This is the most luxurious of all court surfaces because it has to be watered, it has to be fertilized, and it has to be mowed. However, it produces the most luxurious tennis play. Tennis skill at its keenest will be seen on grass surfaces. A grass court tournament tempo produces a ''fast'' ball. The ball stays low to the surface when it bounces. This gives the player minimum time to execute his strokes. ''You only need a BIG serve and volley game on grass courts,'' Morey vows.

Wimbledon's All England Club and Forest Hills' West Side Tennis Club were the two most famous grass court surfaces in the tennis world. However, Forest Hills changed their grass courts into clay courts for the '75 Forest Hills U.S. Open Tennis Championship.

''All in all, the best surface for a player to develop an 'all weather' tennis game is the cement surface, such as Laykold,'' Morey declares. On the cement surface, the player can play a mixmaster game. He can attack—retrieve—serve a BIG serve—defeat a BIG serve with superior ground strokes.

''This is the surface the Junior tennis player should start on. He can 'round' out his game,'' Morey advises. When a player develops into a champion, he will learn to adjust his game to the ''kind'' of play the surface requires.

Then there is the indoor wooden court. Give a tennis player a choice and he will take the outdoor health advantages of tennis play. But if the weather is bad, the player will storm off to an indoor court.

"Yesteryear's" indoor courts were in gymnasiums with slick, wooden surfaces. The wooden surface is the fastest surface of all. When the ball contacts the wooden surface, it skids and stays low. "If for some reason a player is playing on a wooden surface, he had better bend his knees and get ready for the fast low ball," says Morey.

However, the indoor courts of today have surfaces made from many different materials. Some indoor court surfaces produce a slower ball, such as Grass-text surface. An indoor surface may be cement with a Laykold topping. This produces a fast ball.

"The old wooden indoor gymnasium-type courts are almost a thing of the past, just as the grass courts," Morey asserts.

To be a member of a Junior Davis Cup team is the coveted spot among young players. The Junior Davis Cup teams are boys 16 to 18 years old. In 1971, Jimmy Connors and Rascoe Tanners were teammates on a Junior Davis Cup team. Four years later they are playing in the "championship" circuit. "Remember, lots of today's champions were members of Junior Davis Cup teams," Morey reminds his Junior students.

Each of the 17 USTA sections has Junior Davis Cup teams. Example: The members of the Texas Junior Davis Cup team for the summer of '75 are: 18 year old-Bill Scanlon, Mark Turpin, Dan Valentincic, Tut Bartzen and Reid Freeman; 16 year old-David Zimmerman, Reid Freeman, Leland Futterman, Doug Crawford, David Dowlen, Jeff Turpin and John Low.

The Junior Davis Cup sectional teams are chosen by a Junior Davis Cup sectional chairman. He bases his choice on the player's USTA ranking performance in qualifying tournaments and performance at tennis camps.

Besides the sectional "teams," there is a national Junior Davis Cup team. "The 20 top seeded 16-18 year old boys have a tournament. The top 8 winners qualify for the National Junior Davis Cup team," explains Morey. Not only do these boys win the coveted title, they get their travel expenses. The sectional teams and the national Junior Davis Cup Team compete with each other.

The National Junior Davis Cup team for the summer of '75 was composed of Tony Giammalva, Larry Gottfried, Jai DiLouie, Matt Mitchell, John Austin, John McEnroe, Chris Delaney, and Van Winitsky. "Jai

DiLouie's mother will tell you Jai 'grew up' with the tennis backboard,'' Morey claims. ''That's how Jai got where he is today—by using the tennis backboard to practice grooving his shots.''

Some other important Junior boys' tournaments are: United States Junior Championship Tournament, played in Kalamazoo, Michigan; the United States Junior Clay Court Championship Tournament, played in Louisville, Kentucky; and The United States Junior Hard Court Championship Tournament, played in Burlingame, California.

The major Junior tournaments for girls are: The USTA Girls' 12-14-16 and 18 Championship, played in Philadelphia, Pennsylvania; the 18 year old Girls Intersectional Team Matches; and the coveted Junior Whitman Cup Team Tournaments. The Junior Whitman Cup team was patterned after the boys' Junior Davis Cup Team. Nancy Jeffett, from Dallas, Texas, is the Texas sectional endorser for the state's Junior Whitman Cup Team.

All Junior Championship Tournaments are open to players who have not reached their eighteenth birthday before January 1st in the year of their tournament competition. ''The USLTA sanctioned tournaments are strict about age requirements,'' warns Morey, ''so you had better make sure you understand their datelines.''

Morey reminds his Junior students of the four outstanding adult tournament championships of the world: the Australian, the French, the British and the American. Should a player win all four of these titles in the same season, he has won ''The Grand Slam'' of tennis.

As Morey directs his youth program, he stands with his hands on his hips and hollers, ''O.K., Sam, now start practicing your serve. Bud, you move over to the next court and receive for him. Go no now—get with it!'' Silently Morey is looking for another potential ''Grand Slam'' winner—like Margaret Court or Rod Laver.

Now the National Collegiate Athletic Association is an association that governs intercollegiate activities. The NCAA governs the rules that enable colleges to offer tennis scholarships.

Morey informs his Junior and college students of the *many* available college tennis scholarships.

''With college tuitions and books going up, some tennis scholarships could mean BIG money,'' Morey declares. Most leading colleges and universities offer tennis scholarships. Morey makes sure his students know about them and how to apply for a tennis scholarship.

Morey has some interesting advice for the tough tournament player. "Watch out for TRICKS!" he warns. "One time I was playing a tournament and had my opponent match point on his serve. He found an *old* ball on the court and he served it to me. I hit the ball before I realized what he had done, and my return was a loser. When I started hollering, my opponent grabbed the ball and knocked it out of the stadium. I lost the point." "Remember, if you hit a ball, you have to play it," Morey explains.

Another tip he claims is: "Two men were in a singles tournament. When they were changing courts, one of the players 'accidentally' spilled water on his opponent's racket when they changed courts on an odd game. Of course, in hot weather, if water gets on a racket, the gut strings go to pieces. So, remember, watch out for ANYTHING in a tennis tournament."

"Finally," he tells his students, "play *lots* of tournaments and soon you will wear the champion's crown."

Chapter Ten

TOURNAMENTS

The breath of excitement fills the air during tennis tournament play—whether it be the BIG ONE at Wimbledon, the Boys 18 and 16 held in Kalamazoo, Michigan, or a local sanctioned USTA tournament.

Sighs and applause crack the still silence as the tennis hero or heroes make spectacular shots. The tennis stars are on stage, just as an actor is on stage. The only difference is that a theatrical stage is usually high above the audience, while the tennis stage is down in a hollow setting, with the audience high above on bleachers.

"Tournaments and bullfights are just alike,"Morey affirms. "The stage setting is the same, and someone is going to be killed."

Tournament play and "fun" play are as different as Gatorade and buttermilk. The main difference in tournament play is the psychological pressure. Competitiveness is intensified. "In tournament play, a player is quick to learn the answers to what he is doing WRONG—that he should be doing RIGHT. Then he can march to the tennis backboard and polish his tarnished mistakes," states Morey.

Entering tournaments will improve your game, whether you are young or old. "After about 30 tournaments, a player will get tournament tough," explains Morey. To be 'tournament tough' means a player becomes tempered physically and mentally. He learns not to tighten up and let competitive pressure bother him. "Those first 30 tournaments are practice tournaments—like backboard practice. You gotta learn," says Morey.

Tournament tennis is a whole new ballgame. So Morey advises his students to enter the tournaments as soon as possible. He starts them in the ten year old division—then the twelve year old—next the fourteen, sixteen and eighteen year old divisions—and finally into the men's and women's adult tournaments.

Morey encourages his 'serious' students to play in tournaments that are SANCTIONED by the *United States Tennis Association* and *State Associations*. The results of a sanctioned USTA tournament are sent to the national and state tennis sections. This is the way a player is ranked in the state and national rankings.

To belong to the USTA, a player buys a USTA membership card.

The USTA annual membership categories and costs are: (1) Life Membership—$200, tax deductible; (2) Husband and Wife Membership—$13.50, plus 12 issues of *Tennis U.S.A.*; (3) Adult Membership (21 and over)—$8.00, plus 12 issues of *Tennis U.S.A.*; (4) Junior Membership (under 21)—$5.50, plus 12 issues of *Tennis U.S.A.*; (5) Junior Membership (under 21)—$3.00, without magazine.

A player may buy his membership card at a tournament or through a tennis club. He will be given a membership number with a receipt. This receipt number will entitle him to play until he receives his membership card with his number from the USTA.

A player is required to use his membership number on his entry blank, in all USTA sanctioned tournaments. His membership number may be renewed the next year.

After the player has filled in his entry blank, he should send the entry to the specified address of the proposed tournament he wishes to enter. All tournaments have an ENTRY DEADLINE. "Better watch it," warns Morey. "If a player's entry is late, he will not be in the tournament."

"If a player doesn't want to be ranked—but wants to play better tennis, play in local tournaments. Tournament play is a MUST, if you want to improve your game," Morey advises.

There are two types of tennis players: AMATEURS and PROFESSIONALS. Professionals play for money—amateurs do not. Tennis has turned from 'petty cash' to 'big money.' So turning 'pro' has become a popular tennis attraction.

A tennis player begins his professional tennis journey by practicing and working hard at backboard practice, court practice, and tournament practice. He must work hard through the use of the sanctioned USTA tournaments until he is ranked high in his region. This will earn him the entrance to play in satellite tournaments or a qualifying tournament. If he wins the satellite tournament, he has qualified himself to play in the regular USTA tournament, where tournament prizes may be trophies *and money*, making him a professional.

Remember, a professional tennis player makes tennis his profession. He plays for money; however, amateurs don't play for money—they play for fun. They play for trophies; they play for the healthful recreational benefits; and they play for the love of the game.

Now there are different kinds of tennis tournaments, such as: (1) court's surface—whether it be clay court, grass court, hard court; (2) tournaments are categorized—whether the tournament will be doubles or singles, or both; (3) different age divisions; (4) open tournaments—tournaments in which amateurs and professionals compete. Many celebrity tournaments are open tournaments; and finally, (4) professional tournaments.

If a tennis club or any organization wants to promote a sanctioned USTA tournament, they first decide what kind of tournament the want. Then they check with their geographical section. There are 17 USTA sections. They are: (1) Eastern—30 E. 42nd Street, N.Y., N.Y. 10017; (2) Florida—46 N.E. 6th Street, Miami, Florida 33132; (3) Intermountain—P.O. Box 2009, Salt Lake City, Utah 84110; (4) Hawaii—94-010 Hokupalemo Place, Mililani Town, Hawaii 96789; (5) Middle Atlantic—3035 Edgewood Avenue, Baltimore, Maryland 21234; (6) Middle States, 3 Club Lane, Reading, Pa. 19607; (7) Missouri Valley—3415 Witmer Parkway, Des Moines, Iowa 50310; (8) New England—P.O. Box 223, Needham, Mass. 02192; (9) Northern California—P.O. Box 337, Moraga, Calif. 94556; (10) Northwestern—975 Northwestern Bank Building, Minneapolis, Minn. 55402; (11) Western—Cincinnati, Ohio 45200; (12) Pacific N.W.—2753 West 29th Avenue, Vancouver, 8, B.C., Canada; (13) Puerto Rico—Box 1813, Hato Rey, Puerto Rico 00936; (14) Southern—3121 Maple Drive, N.E., Room 21B, Atlanta, Georgia 30305; (15) Southern California—609 Cahuenga Blve., Los Angeles, Calif. 90004;

(16) Southwestern—405 Lawyers Title Bldg., Tucson, Arizona 85701; (17) Texas—P.O. Box 192, Austin, Texas 78767.

If the regional section where a request for a tournament is made does not have a tournament sanctioned at that particular date, the USTA sectional division will grant the date and give their sanction to the requested tournament.

After a club or an organization has been given the "go ahead" signal, the club promoting the tournament sends ENTRY blanks to other members of tennis clubs, country clubs, schools and known top seeded players that are in their USTA section. The entry blanks will declare the fee, the dates, the kind of tournament, and other pertinent information with the return DEADLINE date.

"Those top-ranked players are looking for tournaments like a hungry bird looks for food—they have tournament fever," declares Morey.

Now as the entry blanks return, the players are seeded according to USTA rules and rankings. Then the "draw" or the decision of the order in which the players will play is done and the tournament plunges into action.

If a local tennis club does not want a sanctioned tournament, they proceed by their own rules and set up the kind of tournament their members want.

Wimbledon's Championship Tennis Tournament is the coveted title desired by all tennis champion professionals. It is the GRAND DAD of all tennis tournaments.

Years ago Wimbledon was founded by four wise men—Julian Marshall, Henry Jones, C.G. Heathcote and J.H. Walsh. They viewed the grandiose turf of The All England Croquet Club at Wimbledon and decided it would be excellent for the new gutsy game of tennis that was sweeping England. These four men realized that lawn tennis rules needed tightening up, so they promoted the idea of re-writing phases of Major Wingefield's rules, plus other tennis rules that were causing confusion. They were successful in their promotion and staged an amateurs' tournament on July 9, 1877, at The All England Croquet Club at Wimbledon.

These four men were responsible for the birth of the now favorite Wimbledon Championship Tournaments in London, England. Now between courts, on the grounds at Wimbledon, are scattered tables with a variety of colored canvas umbrellas, where one might sit and sip tea." The center court is walled in with a black iron fence. Long wooden flower boxes are attached to the fence. In the spring, the boxes unfold a lovely variety of white, yellow, orange and red flowers. Under the flower boxes are plump green shrubbery that adds more beauty to the regal setting.

No wonder the tennis world chose Wimbledon as its top tennis tournament.

Another classic tournament is the Davis Cup. This tournament is different in that it is acquired through teamwork and is considered international competition.

The Davis Cup founders were four Harvard men. They wer Malcom Whitman, Beals Wright, Holcombe Ward and Dwight F. Davis. These four men left New York on August 24, 1899 for the West Coast to challenge the Hardy brothers and the Whitney brothers. It was an East versus West match. The four Harvard men won, and their success convinced Dwight F. Davis that "international flavor" would foster the tennis game.

Dwight Davis won the USNLTA approval. He then ordered a Boston silversmith to make a 13-inch high sterling silver bowl that became known as the Davis Cup. Now international competition could be open to the world. On February 21, 1900, a British team was defeated by the American team at the Longwood Cricket Club in Boston. So the Davis Cup remained in America, untarnished by the brittle British.

Soon the Davis Cup's international flavor found teams competing for the cup from New Zealand, Austria, and Belgium. Then other countries organized their teams. The Davis Cup gave tennis a patriotic cloak.

To be on the American Davis Cup team, a player has to be chosen by the Captain of the Davis Cup team. The USTA has a committee that picks the team's captain. Then the captain has the authority to pick whom and as many players as he wants. Tony Tradert is today's Davis Cup team captain. The Davis Cup has not been in America for the past few years. However, on August 30, 1975, Jimmy Connors announced he would play for Tony Tradert on the Davis Cup team. So America expects a quick return of the Davis Cup.

"Now remember," reminds Morey, "those players who play championship tennis at Wimbledon or are on the Davis Cup team, became TOURNAMENT TOUGH."

Chapter Eleven

RULES OF THE GAME

"If you don't know the rules of a game, how can you play the game?" Morey asks.

The following statements are a True and False quiz for the rules of tennis as sanctioned by the USLTA. The right answers follow the quiz.

THE SINGLES GAME

Rule 1

The court shall be a rectangle, 79 feet long and 27 feet wide. It shall be divided across the middle by a net. The height of the net shall be 3 feet at the center. T__ F__

Rule 2

The permanent fixtures of the court shall include only the net, posts, cord or metal cable, strap and band. T__ F__

Rule 3

The ball shall have uniform outer surface and shall be more than two and one-half inches and less than two and five-eights inches in diameter. T__ F__

Rule 4

Server and Receiver

The players shall stand on opposite sides of the net; the player who first delivers the ball shall be called the server, and the other the receiver. The receiver must stand within the lines bounding his court. T__ F__

Rule 5

Choice of Sides and Service

The choice of sides and the right to be Server or Receiver in the first game shall be decided by toss. The player winning the toss may choose, or require his opponent to choose:

(a) The right to be Server or Receiver, in which case the other player shall choose the side; or

(b) The side, in which case the other player shall choose the right to be Server or Receiver. T__ F__

Rule 6

Delivery of Service

In a singles game a server may stand behind the base line between the side line for singles and side line of doubles. In other words, the server may stand behind the base line of the alley used in the doubles game. T__ F__

A player may serve underhand. T__ F__

Rule 7

Foot Fault

The Server shall, throughout the delivery of the service:

(a) Not change his position by walking or running;

(b) Not touch, with either foot, any area other than that behind the base line within the imaginary extension of the center-mark and side line. T__ F__

Rule 8

From Alternate Courts

The ball served shall pass over the net and hit the ground within the

Service Court which is diagonally opposite, but not on any line bounding such Court, before the Receiver returns it. T__ F__

Rule 9

Faults

The Service is a fault:

(a) If the Server commit any breach of Rules 6, 7 or 8;

(b) If he misses the ball in attempting to strike it;

(c) If the ball served touches a permanent fixture (other than the net, strap or band) before it hits the ground. T__ F__

After throwing a ball up preparatory to serving, the Server decides not to strike at it and catches it instead. Is it a fault? T__ F__

Rule 10

Service After a Fault

After a fault (if it be the first fault), the Server shall serve again from behind the same half of the Court from which he served that fault. T__ F__

Rule 11

The Server does not have to wait until the Receiver is ready for his second serve. T__ F__

Rule 12

A Let

In all cases where a let has to be called under the rules, or to provide for an interruption to play, it shall have the following interpretations:

(a) When called solely in respect of a service, that one service only shall be replayed.

(b) When called under any other circumstances, the point shall be replayed. T__ F__

Rule 13

The Service is a Let

The Service is a Let:

(a) If the ball served touches the net, strap or band, and is otherwise good, or after touching the net, strap or band, touches the Receiver or anything which he wears or carries before hitting the ground.

(b) If a service or a fault be delivered when the Receiver is not ready. T__ F__

Rule 14

When Receiver Becomes Server

At the end of the first game the Receiver shall become the Server, and the Server Receiver; and so on alternately in all the subsequent games of a match. If a player serves out of turn, he loses his next turn to serve. T__ F__

Rule 15

Ball in Play Till Point Decided

A ball is in play from the moment at which it is delivered in service. Unless a fault or a let be called, it remains in play until the point is decided. T__ F__

Rule 16

Server Wins Point

The server does not win the point:

(a) If the ball served, not being a let under Rule 13, touch the Receiver or anything which he wears or carries, before it hits the ground;

(b) If the Receiver otherwise loses the point as provided by Rule 18. T__ F__

Rule 17

Receiver Wins Point

The receiver wins the point:

(a) If the Server serves two consecutive faults;

(b) If the Server otherwise loses the point as provided by Rule 18. T__ F__

Rule 18

Player Loses Point

A player loses the point if:

(a) He fails, before the ball in play has hit the ground twice consecutively, to return it directly over the net (except as provided in Rule 22 (a) or (c); or

(b) He returns the ball in play so that it hits the ground, a permanent fixture or other object, outside any of the lines which bound his opponent's Court (except as provided in Rule 22 (a) and (c); or

(c) He volleys the ball and fails to make a good return even when standing outside the Court; or

(d) He touches or strikes the ball in play with his racket more than once in making a stroke; or

(e) He or his racket (in his hand or otherwise) or anything which he wears or carries touch the net posts, cord or metal cable, strap or band or the ground within his opponent's Court at any time while the ball is in play; or

(f) He volleys the ball before it has passed the net; or

(g) The ball in play touches him or anything that he wears or carries, except his racket in his hand or hands; or

(h) He throws his racket at and hits the ball. T__ F__

Rule 19

Player Hinders Opponent

A player may commit any act to hinder his opponent as long as the player does not hurt his opponent. T__ F__

Rule 20

Ball Falling on Line—Good

A ball falling on a line is regarded as falling in the Court bounded by that line. T__ F__

Rule 21

Ball Touching Permanent Fixture

If the ball in play touches a permanent fixture (other than the net, posts, cord or metal cable, strap or band) after it has hit the ground, the player who struck it loses the point; if before it hits the ground, his opponent wins the point. T__ F__

Rule 22

Good Return

It is a good return:

(a) If the ball touches the net, posts, cord or metal cable, strap or band, provided that it passes over any of them and hits the ground within the Court; or

(b) If the ball, served or returned, hits the ground within the proper Court and rebound or is blown back over the net, and the player whose turn it is to strike reach over the net and play the ball, provided that neither he nor any part of his clothes or racket touch the net, posts, cord or metal cable, strap or band or the ground within his opponent's court, and that the stroke be otherwise good; or

(c) If the ball be returned outside the post, either above or below the level of the top of the net, even though it touches post, provided that it hits the ground within the proper Court; or

(d) If a player's racket pass over the net after he has returned the ball, provided the ball pass the net before being played and be properly returned; or

(e) If a player succeeded in returning the ball, served or in play, which strikes a ball lying in the Court. T__ F__

Rule 23

Interference

In case a player is hindered in making is hindered in making a stroke by anything not within his control except a permanent fixture of the Court, or except as provided for in Rule 19, the point shall not be replayed. T__ F__

Rule 24

The Game

If a player wins his first point, the score is called 15 for that player; on winning his second point, the score is called 30 for that player; on winning his thrid point, the score is called 40 for that player. And the fourth point won by a player is scored game for that player except as below:

If both players have won three points, the score is called deuce, and the next point won by a player is called advantage for that player. If the same player wins the next point, he wins the game; if the other player wins the next point the score is again called deuce; and so on until a player wins the two points immediately following the score at deuce, when the game is scored for that player. T__ F__

Rule 25

The Set

A player (or players) who first wins 5 games wins a set; except that he must win by a margin of two games over his opponent and where necessary, a set shall be extended until this margin be achieved. T__ F__

Rule 26

When Players Change Sides

The players shall change sides at the end of the first, third and subsequent alternate game of each set, and at the end of each set unless the total number of games in such set be even, in which case the change is not made until the end of the first game of the next set. T__ F__

Rule 27

Maximum Number of Sets

The maximum number of sets in a match shall be seven, or, where women take part, four. T__ F__

Rule 28

Rules Apply to Both Sexes

Except where otherwise stated, every reference in these Rules to the masculine includes the feminine gender. T__ F__

Rule 29

Decisions of Umpire and Referee

In matches where an Umpire is appointed, his decision shall be final; but where a Referee is appointed, an appeal shall lie to him from the decision of an Umpire on a question of law, and in all such cases the decision of the Referee shall be final, except that in Davis Cup matches the decision of a linesman can be changed by the Referee, or by the Umpire with the consent of the Referee.

The Referee, in his discretion, may at any time postpone a match on account of darkness or the condition of the ground or the weather. In any case of postponement the previous score and previous occupancy of Courts shall hold good, unless the Referee and the players unanimously agree otherwise. T__ F__

Rule 30

Play shall be continuous from the first service till the match be concluded unless all players agree to a period of time for rest. T__ F__

THE DOUBLES GAME

Rule 31

The above Rules shall apply to the Doubles Game except as below. T__ F__

Rule 32

Dimension of Court

For the Doubles Game, the court shall be 36 feet in width, i.e., 4½ feet wider on each side that the Court for the Singles Game, and those portions of the singles side lines which lie between the two service lines shall be called the service side lines. In other respects, the Court shall be similar to that described in Rule 1, but the portions of the singles side lines between the base line and service line on each side of the net may be omitted if desired. T__ F__

Rule 33

The order of serving in doubles is done by each pair flipping a coin. The partner of the pair who served in the first game shall serve in the third game. The partner of the player who served in the second game shall serve in the fourth, and so on in the same order in all subsequent games of a set. T__ F__

Rule 34

Order of Receiving

The order of receiving the service shall be decided at the beginning of each set as follows:

The pair who have to receive the service in the first game shall decide which partner shall receive the first service, and that partner shall continue to receive the first service in every odd game throughout that set. The opposing pair shall likewise decide which partner shall receive the first service in the second game and that partner shall continue to receive the first service in every even game throughout that set. Partners shall receive the service alternately throughout each game. T__ F__

Rule 35

Service Out of Turn

If a partner serve out of his turn, the pair do not alter the mistake, but rather change their service turns and play accordingly. T__ F__

Rule 36

Error in Order of Receiving

If during a game the order of receiving the service is changed by the receivers, it shall remain as altered until the end of the game in which the mistake is discovered, but the partners shall resume their original order of receiving in the next game of that set in which they are receivers of the service. T__ F__

Rule 37

Ball Touching Server's Partner is Fault

The service is a fault as provided by Rule 9, or if the ball served touch the Server's partner or anything he wears or carries, but if the ball served touch the partner of the Receiver or anything which he wears or carries, not being a let under Rule 13(a), before it hits the ground, the Server wins the point. T__ F__

Rule 38

Ball Struck Alternately

The ball shall be struck alternately by one or other player of the opposing pairs and if a player touches the ball in play with his racket in contravention of this Rule, his opponents win the point. T__ F__

"Now that you have the Rules for the game of tennis, don't forget the Rule for the tennis backboard—PRACTICE," states Morey.

ANSWERS TO TRUE AND FALSE QUIZ

1. False
2. False
3. True
4. False
5. True
6. False
   (a) True
7. True
8. False
9. True
   (a) False
10. True
11. False
12. True
13. True
14. False
15. True
16. False
17. True
18. True
19. False
20. True
21. False
22. True
23. False
24. True

25. False
26. True
27. False
28. True
29. True
30. False
31. True
32. True
33. False
34. True
35. False
36. True
37. True
38. True

Chapter Twelve

PROOF OF THE PUDDING

The proof of the pudding is not found in the boiling pot on the stove, but rather at the table where it is served. The proof comes when you "taste" the pudding. It is either smooth and tasty or lumpy and untasty.

"The tennis backboard is an excellent tennis tool for improving your game—and here's my "tasting" proof. You'll find it smooth and tasty," chuckles Morey.

First let's take a quick glimpse of an international flavor and see what the amorous French and other foreigners say about the tennis backboard.

Monique Bensusan, from France Federation of Lawn Tennis, explains, "In France almost all tennis clubs of any importance have one or several training walls or tennis backboards." The French tennis player believes that playing against the wall is an agreeable means of training and perfecting one's game without an opponent. They believe backboard practice helps the player keep his eye on the ball, builds leg muscles, and develops better coordination. However, the Frenchmen believe as Morey does—that the student must have adequate instruction before he goes to the backboard so the player will not develop bad habits—which are always difficult to correct. "The French players exercise often on the training walls," states Monique Bensusan.

Across the globe where the leprechauns live, Terry Gleeson said the

Sutton Lawn Club, Dublin, Ireland, has a tennis backboard and is used by the Irish tennis player whenever the tennis courts are full. Keven Newton was Ireland's No. 1 seeded player, and Terry said Newton did practice on the tennis backboard.

A Swedish tennis pro for "Adventure's Camp" in Wisconsin, Ulf Stenbom, said, "In Sweden, backboards have been used for many years as an effective teaching aid. Backboard usage seems to be spreading throughout Europe."

In the Orient, we have Nana Sato, a young Japanese tennis player. Nana was in Tyler, Texas, in March of '75. She came to play in the McFarlin Womens' Tennis Circuit, a satellite tournament for the Virginia Slims. Nana highly endorsed the tennis backboard and said, "The tennis backboards and walls from brick buildings are in wide use in Japan, because Japan has so few tennis courts." Then she added, "It is not unusual for one to stand on a court in Japan and wait for several sets of tennis to be played before you can get a court."

"That's why they use the backboard so much," explains Morey. "They had rather play than wait."

Then on the British Isles, close to London, you will find The All England Lawn Tennis and Croquet Club—more commonly called Wimbeldon. Here the most prestigious of all the tough tennis tournaments are staged. On the grounds of Wimbeldon, you may now see a tennis backboard. C.J. Corringer, assistant secretary at the club, explains, "We have recently built a tennis backboard and it is used by the club members. A great number of clubs throughout the country do have practice walls—whether they be of brickwork, concrete or wood."

"So you see, the tennis backboard isn't just 'All American'—it has lots of FOREIGN BLOOD in it too," Morey insists.

Meanwhile, back in our own country, Terry Holiday from La Jolla, California, was victorious and won a Virginia Slim Satellite in February of '75. Terry advocates the tennis backboard practice. She says, "It is great for stroke concentration and footwork."

Carleton Billups, an adult student of Morey's, said, "I went to Morey—took a couple of lessons from him, then went to the backboard. It trains your timing, your eye, and your coordination. You learn more RAPIDLY." Then Carleton explains that he is buildiing a hunting lodge in

Mississippi, and he is including tennis courts and a tennis backboard for his grandchildren.

"That's what parents and grandparents *should* do for their grandchildren," Morey adds.

A tennis pro at North Wood Country Club in Dallas, Texas, Bob Mooty's comments on the tennis backboard were, "It is excellent practice. The problem is picking the student most likely to develop into a top player and getting him to use it."

When asked how he overcame that problem, he answered, "I teach them to set a goal, and once they hit 500 balls without a miss, you can't keep the students away."

Bobby McKinley, the tennis coach at Trinity University in San Antonio, Texas, explains, "I think the tennis backboard is excellent for beginners—but not for the highly advanced player."

"It certainly can't hurt an advanced player," Morey quickly adds.

Now let's look at some good-tasting, FLASHY puddings—none other than the "flashy" handsome Australian, John Newcombe, who says, "Some backboards are *very* helpful to practice against, but sometimes they are too small to be of real benefit."

Morey is quick to agree with John.

Lamar Hunt, a director in World Championship Tennis in Dallas, Texas, states, "I personally use a backboard and enjoy it."

Mr. Hunt asked WCT Executive Director, Mike Davies, who is a former pro and former member of the British Davis Cup Team, to give his comments on the tennis backboard.

Michael Davies replied, "I am an advocate of anything that helps get a player to have a racket in his hand and hit a ball. I feel that this way they can not only learn how a tennis ball reacts with the spin off the wall, etc., but they can quicken their reflexes and generally get the feel of hitting a tennis ball—which is not the most natural thing in the world to do."

Mike Davies went a step further and warned, "As the player progresses, of course, he should be cautioned against getting into sloppy habits, which is very easy on a backboard. All training on the backboard should be in a concentrated time period, and as soon as it gets sloppy, then it is of little use. Practicing volleying only against a backboard is good for reflexes, for firming up the muscles in the wrist and hands, and eye

(Above) Forehand stroke

(Below) Stewart Haberle practicing forehand ground stroke

(Above) Stewart Haberle practicing backhand ground stroke

(Below) Stewart Haberle with instructor

coordination. However, all in all, I'm a complete advocate of the backboard.''

Here is still more ''good-tasting'' pudding.

When Arthur Ashe, the 1975 Wimbeldon Tennis Champion, was asked if he advocated tennis backboard practice, he replied, ''Backboards are excellent for *Footwork practice* and *grooving strokes through rapid repetition.*''

Morey, hacking a chuckle of approval, says, ''See, that's what I've been saying all along.''

When Morey's friend, Don Budge, who is a director and pro at Don Budge Tennis Club in Brentwood, New York, was contacted for his comments on the tennis backboard, he replied, ''Yes, I am a great advocate of the backboard for practice. We do have a big one at my tennis camp.''

The response of Henry A. Talbert, Jr., National Tennis Coordinator of the United States Lawn Tennis Association, on the tennis backboard, was, ''We have found the backboard an excellent way to teach the following: (1) Forehand, backhand, serve, volley and overhead smash; (2) Footwork and alignment; and (3) The concept of timing, pace and stroke conditioning (grooving shots).''

''In short,'' he adds, ''the backboard is an excellent tool in teaching tennis. Its cost is minimal to construct and, depending on its size, it can accommodate many students. Finally, it is also a good way to stimulate low level competition that is transferable to the game of tennis.''

Still more tasty pudding comes from Pancho Gonzales ''himself.'' Pancho's comments on the tennis backboard were, ''I do feel that it is important for beginners to be able to hit as many balls as possible. This is how they can become well acquainted with the range of bounces a ball will take. Therefore, backboards can be very helpful.

However, to develop a more grooved swing that will be consistent, a player should be involved with actual tennis competition.''

The comments of Tex Schwab, president of the United States Professional Tennis Association, Inc., concerning the backboard, brought a ''different taste'' to the pudding. Tex firmly professes, ''For many years I have been one of the most violent opponents to backboard teaching—except in the case of accomplished players. I could never see how a beginner could do anything but get into very bad habits because of the pace with which tennis balls come off the backboard. We all realize that balance and footwork are the secrets to developing good strokes, and backboard practice never gave a beginner sufficient time to prepare.''

Morey's reply to Tex Schwab is, ''To each his own—but it's obvious I have more backboard *believers* than non-believers.''

Now let's ''taste'' the last two comments. Our own likeable, agreeable and lovable Bud Collins replied with a fond memory, ''I used the sidewall (brick) of Central School, Berea, Ohio, to start off as a hacker. My lifetime record vs. the wall is 0-21,827. However, I think it was very good for the reflexes.''

Finally, we have a favorable comment from Cliff Drysdale, pro at Lakeway World of Tennis, Austin, Texas.

Cliff said, ''I am a great believer in the tennis backboard. I personally spent many hours a day on the backboard when I was starting out on the game, and my advice to any parents who have aspiring young tennis players in the family is, in fact, to make available to them a tennis racket, balls and a backboard. This does not mean that they should force them to play, but only that they should make it possible for them to do so.''

Morey thinks Cliff Drysdale's advice to parents with aspiring young tennis players is sound—but he goes a step further. The parents could be aspiring tennis players and they could also share this excellent tennis tool—the backboard.

''There is no substitute for the good 'taste' in tennis that comes with backboard practice,'' Morey reaffirms, as he practices his volley shots in front of the BIG GREEN WALL—a tennis backboard.

ACKNOWLEDGMENTS

For the many letters and helpful suggestions as to where we might find certain information, we want to thank The United States Lawn Tennis Association.

Too, we appreciate their permission to quote from their *Official USLT Yearbook-75Bc and the United States Lawn Tennis Official Encyclopedia of Tennis.*

Illustration Credit:

Black and White Photos—Bob Delk Photographers
Architectural Constructions—David Fair
Art Sketches—Wynn Watson

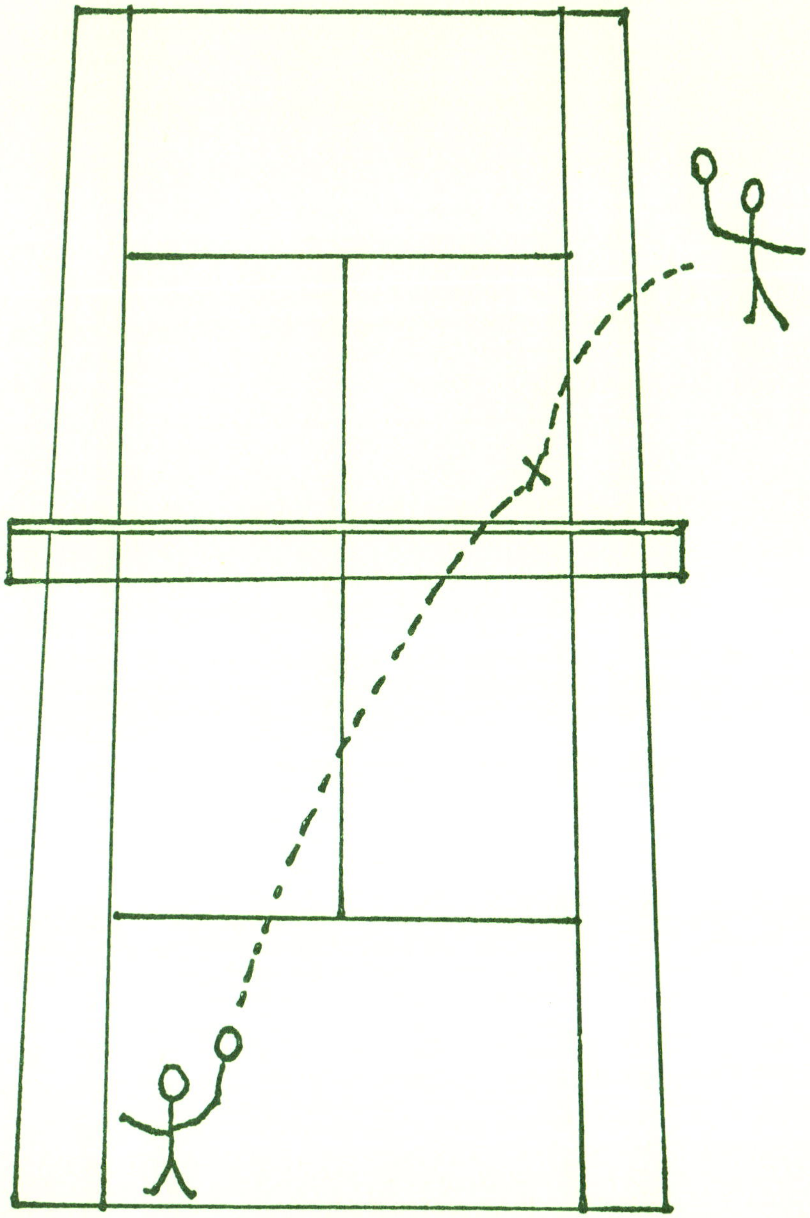

Pulling your opponent out of position

(Opposite page) Drop shot (Above) Lob

ILLUSTRATIONS